Rueinschneider 12/85

Oblique Contexts

LEONARD LINSKY

Oblique Contexts

The University of Chicago Press
Chicago and London

LEONARD LINSKY is a professor of philosophy at
the University of Chicago. He is the editor of two
books—*Semantics and the Philosophy of Language*
and *Reference and Modality*—and the author of
two—*Referring* and *Names and Descriptions*.

The University of Chicago Press, Chicago 60637
The University of Chicago Press, Ltd., London

Library of Congress Cataloging in Publication Data

Linsky, Leonard.
Oblique contexts.

Bibliography: p. 165
Includes index.
1. Meaning (Philosophy)—History—20th century.
2. Frege, Gottlob, 1848–1925.   3. Russell, Bertrand,
1872–1970.   I. Title.
B840.L538   1983   121′.68   82–23825
ISBN 0–226–48439–4

For my son,
Bernard Linsky

Io credo chi'ei credette chi'io credesse . . .
Dante

Our subject is logic . . .
Alonzo Church

Contents

Preface

I had planned to include a chapter on propositional attitudes in my book *Names and Descriptions* (1977). I kept postponing work on that topic, however, because I was then fully absorbed in the subject of the metaphysical (alethic) modalities and the complex of problems connected with them dealt with in Saul Kripke's published lectures "Naming and Necessity" (Kripke, [NN]).* The two topics of alethic modality and the propositional attitudes ought to be treated together, I thought at that time. The syntactic and semantic features of both classes of modalities, which set them apart as special, are so similar that I assumed that a uniform theory, with but minor adjustments for the differences, would be forthcoming. In the meantime, I worked away at necessity and possibility, at Aristotelian essentialism and rigid designation, with the idea that, if I could manage to achieve clarity about the issues connected with these subjects, it would be mainly a matter of following out the analogies to arrive at a similar position with regard to belief. My attitude was only reinforced by the current occupation with possible-worlds semantics as a uniform approach to the whole area of nonextensional contexts, including alethic modality, propositional attitudes, and counterfactuals.

Thus I postponed the study of belief and assertion until the rest of my book was finished. When I finally turned to the neglected topics, however, my previous expectations were shattered. The subject now seemed to be far more difficult than I had supposed it would be. The analogies upon which I was relying went lame when I pushed them. I found myself with what I thought was a clear view of the philosoph-

---

* I will use abbreviations of this kind in citations. Full publication data will be found in the Bibliography.

ical problems connected with alethic modality, and I was convinced that I knew how best to deal with them; but the corresponding problems of the propositional attitudes now seemed even more intractable when seen against the background of what I thought was a successful treatment of more narrowly logical modalities. Possible-worlds semantics worked fine for necessity and possibility, I found, but not at all well for belief, and nothing else seemed to work either. In the end, two courses were open to me: either I could alter my original project by leaving out any treatment of intensional contexts other than those involving necessity or I could abandon the idea of publishing the work at all. I decided to publish the work already finished, and it appeared under the title *Names and Descriptions*.

In the meantime I had been elected president of the American Philosophical Association (Western Division). My principal task was to prepare an address for its annual meeting. I decided to present an account of my unsuccessful efforts to deal with belief, so that at least some negative lessons might be learned, even though I still had little of a positive nature to communicate. The result was my paper on "Believing and Necessity" (Linsky, [BN]). The work for that address turned out to be the start of the present book; it is included here as chapter 5. My preparation for this paper convinced me that I should abandon the possible-worlds approach to propositional attitudes, and I decided to turn back instead for a closer study of the intensional logics of Frege and Russell, which constitute the historical background of current work in this area. The more I studied this work, the more I came to admire the subtlety, richness, and sophistication of these pioneering approaches to the problems that concerned me. Indeed, these classical theories seemed to be superior to any of their more recent alternatives, and I became more and more fascinated with the project of making a thorough comparison of these two theories of meaning, each of which seemed so powerful and yet totally opposed to the other. As a result of this study I came to see that what was required for a successful account of belief and the other propositional attitudes was work at a more fundamental level than that carried out by those developing the possible-worlds approach. One finds, for example, in the classical presentation of this point of view provided in Hintikka's *Knowledge and Belief* (Hintikka, [*KB*]) formulas such as "$B_a p$" ("a believes that p") "$K_a p$" ("a knows that

p "), "$(\exists x)K_a(x = b)$" ("a knows who b is") and its doxastic analogue "$(\exists x)B_a(x = b)$". One is then told that 'a' and 'b' stand for
names of persons and that 'p' holds a place for a declarative sentence.
But one is never told what, if anything, these sentences denote. Do
they denote propositions (Russell, Frege), or truth-values, or utter-
ances? Or are they used autonomously to denote themselves? We are
never told, in other words, what are the *objects* of the attitudes.
Consequently, Hintikka's system does not allow for quantification
over these objects. We cannot, within this system, formulate even
such apparent quantifications as this: 'Aristotle is sometimes mistaken'. (This observation I owe to C. Anthony Anderson,
[SNALSD], pp. 231–32, n. 1.)

The first task, then, is to provide an account of the *logical form*
of intensional contexts. The next step would involve the construction
of a *theory* for them, based on special axioms such as Hintikka's
(although Hintikka's work, within the framework of possible-worlds
semantics, produces systems of "doxastic logic" in which the concept of belief is so idealized as to be only remotely associated with
our actual conception). Whatever such a theory will finally look like,
it is with this preliminary question of logical form that I deal in this
work. Consequently, nothing here turns on whether we speak of
belief rather than, say, assertion or any other propositional attitude.
Such distinctions will be relevant at the next stage, when one attempts
to construct a full theory of these concepts, but not here. It is,
however, my belief that the most interesting philosophical issues
connected with these topics are located at this more fundamental
level. (In distinguishing these parts in a full account of belief, I
follow Alonzo Church's statement in "Logic and Analysis": "I shall
hold that a full analysis must consist of three things, a logic of belief,
a theory based on special postulates, and an account of the obser-
vational criteria for recognizing or testing belief" [Church, [LA],
p. 79].)

There is another important component in a full account of the
propositional attitudes that is not dealt with in this work. I do not
attempt to provide an answer to the question 'Under what empirical
conditions are we justified in asserting of someone that he believes
(knows, asserts, etc.,) that p?' One person may say 'London is
beautiful' under certain circumstances and thereby express his belief

that London is beautiful; another person may say these same words and not believe that London is beautiful. What empirically testable conditions must be satisfied to warrant our assertion that the first person but not the second actually believes what he says? Neither Russell nor Frege discusses this question, and, so far as I know, nobody has provided a satisfactory answer to it. I do not attempt to answer the question. Our lack of understanding here can produce a certain skepticism about the entire topic of the attitudes. Are we saying anything at all precise when we attribute a belief to another or to ourselves? Does *anything* about *A*'s beliefs follow from the assertion that *A* believes that *p*? I must admit to a strong tendency to share this skepticism, but I do not deal with these issues here. For the purpose of the present work, it is assumed that statements of the form '*A* believes that *p*' are meaningful; it is also assumed that a single person, *A*, may believe that Cicero denounced Catiline and not believe that Tully denounced Catiline because *A* does not realize that Cicero and Tully are the same man. For our purposes it is not necessary to give an account of how we might verify or confirm, by an empirical test, the statement that *A* does believe that Cicero denounced Catiline and does not believe that Tully denounced Catiline. I do not need to make any further assumptions about belief in order to determine what (if anything) follows about what *A* believes from the statement that *A* believes that Cicero denounced Catiline. Our investigation can proceed even in the face of the skeptical view that maintains that nothing that turns on the meaning of 'belief' follows with certainty (belief being the kind of concept it is). Indeed, I believe that it is characteristic of our concepts of propositional attitudes—at any rate of our concepts of knowledge, belief, and assertion—that they are vague concepts. It is not clear when they do or do not apply.

I agree with Dummett, who says: "But in fact it is easy to see that there cannot be a *logic* of belief or of knowledge in the ordinary sense at all. . . . This is because belief and knowledge are ineradicably *vague* notions" (Dummett, [*Frege*], p. 285). Then he proposes the following as an adequate test for knowledge and belief: "Roughly speaking, a person believes something to be the case if an expression of that belief can fairly easily be elicited from him by prompting him appropriately; and similarly for knowledge" (ibid., pp. 285–86).

Dummett then observes that a person may, by this criterion, hold inconsistent beliefs; he gives expression to them in different contexts. As to vagueness, Dummett offers the following case: John and Jane are in conversation. There is a fact about Jane that John knows (believes), but perhaps Jane does not know (believe) that John knows (believes). On the other hand, Jane may very well know (believe) that John knows (believes) the relevant fact; but John does not realize that Jane does know (believe) this. But, on the other hand, John may realize this, after all, but perhaps Jane is unaware that John realizes that she knows (believes) he is in possession of this fact about her. We may continue this series without end. In each case John and Jane possess a certain amount of knowledge, but there is some fact that the other does not realize. While any one of the descriptions may fit the facts, it is also possible that *none* of them does. It is possible that there is nothing that the one knows and that the other does not: "everything is open between them." After all, they may even, after a point, have openly discussed the fact in question! "Do they both have an infinite amount of knowledge? Namely, John knows this fact about Jane, and Jane knows that John knows this fact about her, and John knows that Jane knows that John knows this fact about her, and Jane knows that John knows that Jane knows that John knows this fact about her, and so on indefinitely." It seems absurd to attribute an infinite amount of knowledge to each of them on this basis, yet each will acknowledge any of the conjuncts with the other's name as subject in this infinite conjunction as soon as he comprehends it. But the greater the complexity of the conjunct involved, the less likely either is to have formulated it for himself and the more reluctant we are to attribute such knowledge to them, "although we should still feel it misleading to say that he did *not* know it" (Dummett, ibid., p. 287). In spite of this vagueness, the concepts of knowledge and belief are far from useless. These and the other attitudes play an enormous role in our lives, and they give rise to philosophically interesting problems. There is impressive philosophical work dealing with them.

The work of Frege and Russell that here concerns me was done during the period of the beginning of modern logic, between 1879, when Frege's *Begriffsschrift* was published, and 1925, when the second edition of *Principia Mathematica* appeared. A great deal has been done on this foundation in the meantime, so that there now exist logistic formulations of the intensional logics of Frege and Russell that meet contemporary standards of rigor. They are due to Alonzo Church, C. Anthony Anderson, and John Myhill. This book is an examination of the philosophical foundations of this work as found in the writings of Frege and Russell. Others have concentrated their efforts not on improving the classical foundation laid by Frege and Russell but in attacking it as fundamentally mistaken. I want to explain why I remain unconvinced by these criticisms, so I have included discussions of the views of Quine, Kripke, Davidson, and others on the topics about which they have advocated rejection of Frege's or Russell's theories. These two aims then—(1) the presentation and defense of Frege's and Russell's intensional logics and (2) the discussion and evaluation of theories by critics of these older views—have largely determined both the topics and methodology of my book.

The book is organized around the "puzzles" (as Russell called them), paradoxes, and antinomies that confront the attempt to give a systematic account of oblique contexts. Some puzzles are presented, in a preliminary way, in the Introduction, which is also devoted to a discussion of methodological issues. Antinomies are reserved for the Appendix. The first chapter begins with Frege's paradox about identity and presents his solutions (early and late); chapter 2 concerns Russell's contrasting treatment of Frege's puzzle. The Appendix carries on with one of this chapter's principal themes—that *Principia Mathematica* (first edition) is best interpreted as a system of intensional logic. This material is put in an appendix because, although continuity is present, it also digresses somewhat from the main topic of the chapter. Perhaps the most important problem confronting any proposal to take intensions seriously in philosophical analysis is the problem of their individuation. I discuss this matter informally at the end of chapter 2. In chapters 3 and 4 I then return to the task of expounding and comparing the theories of Frege (chapter 3) and Russell (chapter 4) as alternative accounts of the logical form of intensional contexts. In the next three chapters I discuss three important and influential rivals to the classical tradition of Frege and Russell—in chapter 5, Hintikka's theory; in chapter 7, Kripke's theory; and, in chapter 6, Quine's celebrated skepticism about the entire undertaking.

Substantial parts of chapters 4, 5, and 6 have been published previously in somewhat different form. The first four sections of chapter 4 appeared in my article "Substitutivity and Descriptions" in the *Journal of Philosophy,* vol. 63, no. 21 (1966). This material had itself evolved from a still earlier version as chapter 5 of my book *Referring* (copublished in 1967 by Humanities Press, Inc., Atlantic Heights, N.J., and by Routledge & Kegan Paul, Ltd., London). The first four sections of chapter 5 come from my "Believing and Necessity," published in *Proceedings and Addresses of the American Philosophical Association,* vol. 50, no. 6 (1977). Chapter 6, with the exception of the last part of section VII, appeared previously in chapter 6 of my book *Names and Descriptions* (published in 1977 by the University of Chicago Press). It appeared in an even earlier version as "Reference, Essentialism, and Modality," *Journal of Philosophy* 66 (1969):687–700. All three chapters have been partially rewritten, expanded, and corrected, and new material has been added to each of them in the course of adapting them to the present work. Permission to make use of all this material is gratefully acknowledged. The material in section IV of the Appendix quotes and paraphrases *in extenso* from John Myhill's "A Refutation of an Unjustified Attack on the Axiom of Reducibility," which appeared as chapter 5 in the *Bertrand Russell Memorial Volume,* edited by George W. Roberts (published in 1979 by George Allen & Unwin, Ltd., London). Permission from John Myhill and the publishers to use this material is gratefully acknowledged.

For the academic year 1978–79 I received a grant from the National Endowment for the Humanities that freed me from my duties at the University of Chicago to pursue this research. My project was to write a draft of the present book—a comparative study of the theories of meaning of Frege and Russell. At about the same time, I received an invitation from Tel Aviv University to deliver the Yehoshua Bar-Hillel Memorial Lectures for 1978. I decided to combine work on my book with the preparation of these lectures, and my three Bar-Hillel Lectures are here published, in much-altered form, in the first three chapters of this work. Other portions of this book were also presented at other Israeli universities at that time.

I am grateful to the National Endowment for the Humanities for its generous grant in aid of my research, and to The University of

Chicago for its generosity in giving me leave to take up the grant and for supplementing it so that I could take it without loss of income. I wish also to express my gratitude to Tel Aviv University for their invitation to deliver the Bar-Hillel Lectures, and especially to Professor Asa Kasher for making the arrangements for our very pleasant stay in Israel. I thank the members of the audience at those lectures who participated in the exceptionally lively discussions that followed them. After each talk I made notes on the principal topics of the discussions, and these notes formed the basis for revisions and extensions that I made in the work when I took it up again after my return to the United States.

Later I had the honor and good fortune to be chosen as an Albert Einstein Visiting Scholar in the Israel Academy of Sciences and Humanities. My award allowed me to return to Tel Aviv for the spring of 1981 in order to complete my manuscript and to present a seminar on its contents at Tel Aviv University. I wish to express my gratitude to the Israel Academy for enabling me to free myself from other obligations in order to pursue my research under conditions that I found ideal. Again Asa Kasher made practical arrangements for our stay in Israel and was constantly of help during our visit. My wife and I are most grateful to him.

I owe a great debt to Professor Alonzo Church for allowing me to study unpublished writings of his and for the help I have received from his recent publications, especially his address on "Russellian Simple Type Theory" (*American Philosophical Association, Proceedings and Addresses, 1973–74*). This work served to orient my research, and anyone familiar with it will notice its influence here. I was fortunate also to hear Church's address "How Far Can Frege's Intensional Logic Be Represented within Russell's Theory of Descriptions?" delivered at the convention in San Diego of the American Philosophical Association in April, 1979, as part of the Association's centenary celebration of the publication of Frege's *Begriffsschrift*. This address by Church greatly influenced the direction of my work. I wish to thank my friend Terence Parsons for allowing me to use his diagrams for the representation of Frege's hierarchy of senses in chapters 2 and 4. Again, my friend and colleague Bill Tait helped me by discussing many parts of the book over coffee. As important to me as his intellectual aid was his constant encouragement. He conveyed to me his belief that my research was worth doing. The penultimate draft of my manuscript was read by Professors C. Anthony Anderson and Josef Stern. I am very grateful to them for the care they have taken with my work, for their encouragement, and for their suggestions for improvement. I have not always followed these suggestions because, perhaps too often, I preferred to do things *my* way. Nevertheless, my gratitude is genuine. I wish to thank my wife Joan for many hours of work correcting the manuscript for publication.

This kind of work is a rather lonely business. I have worked away at it for years without showing the whole of it to anyone, and I have had my doubts. At times I felt some pride as I read through what I had written. At other times I was plunged into gloom. Then I told myself that my doubts did not matter; I would write this book for myself—record my thoughts on subjects that had long been of interest to me and keep the work as a record of what I had learned. But I could not ever really completely suppress the hope that others would also find my research of value and that one day it would be published. So the encouragement of Tony Anderson and of my colleagues Bill Tait, Alan Donagan, Manley Thompson, Josef Stern, and my students, especially Akeel Bilgrami, all of whom heard parts of the work in progress, presented at departmental meetings, in private discussions, or in classes, was of importance to me, and I thank them for it. In any case, and however it came about, I reached the point, after a while, at which I could not stop short of publishing these thoughts. It is with such mixed feelings that now I do so.

Chicago–Tel Aviv

A Note on the Terms "Intentional" and "Intensional"

A human action is *intentional* as opposed, e.g., to a reflex response, which is involuntary. Brentano held that mental acts are distinguished from physical acts by a trait he characterized as "intentionality" or directedness toward an object. The special manner in which we think of nonexistent objects—as, for example, when we think of Pegasus—exemplifies the intentionality of mental life. The act of thinking of Pegasus is different from the act of thinking of Cerberus; these acts are directed toward different objects. The study of *intentionality* in this sense is a main concern of Brentano, Husserl, and Meinong. It is a branch of philosophical psychology and is perhaps the main concern of phenomenology. Besides thinking, other mental acts characterized by intentionality are belief, assumption, hope. When one believes, assumes, hopes, one believes something, assumes something, and hopes for something. Of course physical acts may also be directed toward an object. When one hits, one hits something. But the manner in which physical acts are directed toward objects is different from the special way in which mental acts are said to have direction toward objects. It is a principal concern of Brentano, Husserl, and Meinong to characterize the nature of this distinguishing feature of psychological phenomena.

The term "intensional" belongs not to philosophical psychology but to logic. It is opposed not to the involuntary or the physical but to "extensional." Terms are said to have both an intension and an extension. The intension of a predicate, e.g., is the meaning expressed by it. The extension of the predicate is the class of things of which the predicate is true. A class may be specified extensionally, e.g., by a list of its members, or intensionally, by giving a property satisfied by all its members and by only them. This property may be thought of as the meaning of a predicate *true of* the objects having that property. The distinction between the intension of a term and its extension may then be extended to other categories of words besides predicates: to proper names, definite descriptions, and even full sentences. According to traditional logic, intensions and extensions obey certain laws. One "law" is that *Intensions determine extensions*. Thus two terms with the same intension are true of the same objects according to this principle. Another purported law, according to the tradition, is that *Intension and extension vary inversely,* so that, the wider the one, the narrower the other.

Without commitment to these or other traditional "laws," the distinction between extension and intension is also used in contemporary logical work. Contexts of assertion, belief, and other propositional attitudes are examples of intensional contexts. The term "oblique contexts" is taken from Frege's name for these contexts, "*ungerade Rede.*" There is, of course, a connection between the intentional idiom and intensionality, for intentional verbs create intensional contexts; but there are intensional contexts that do not involve intentional verbs, e.g., necessity contexts. There is also a contrast between extensional and intensional entities. The extension of a (declarative) sentence is its truth-value; its intension is the proposition it expresses. Classes and concrete individuals are extensions, properties and individual concepts are intensions. Relations *in intension* are contrasted with relations *in extension*—the class of ordered n-tuples that satisfy the relation in intension.

There are also *principles* of extensionality. The axiom of extensionality in set-theory is:

$$(x)(y)[(z)(z \epsilon x \equiv z \epsilon y) \supset (x = y)],$$

in which the bound variables range over sets. This principle identifies coextensive classes. Any principle that identifies coextensive entities is an extensionality principle for entities of that kind; extensional entities are entities that obey an appropriate extensionality principle. Intensional entities do not obey the corresponding extensionality principle. Hence, coextensive intensional entities may nevertheless be different. Functions that always give the same values for the same arguments may still be regarded as different intensionally because of the different *ways* in which they give their values for given arguments. Functions that are identified because, *as functions,* they always yield the same values for the same arguments may still be classified as intensional functions because their values are intensions rather than extensions.

Introduction

A logical theory may be tested by its capacity for dealing with puzzles, and it is a wholesome plan, in thinking about logic, to stock the mind with as many puzzles as possible, since these serve much the same purpose as is served by experiments in physical science.

Bertrand Russell, "On Denoting"

This work is a comparative study of some main features of the theories of meaning of Gottlob Frege and Bertrand Russell. A central feature of its methodology involves taking seriously Russell's advice, quoted above (Russell, [OD], p. 47).* Thus I compare Frege's theory and Russell's by examining their alternative solutions to a number of puzzles involving identity, necessity, intentionality, proper names, and other concepts. Here, in the Introduction, I present some of these puzzles and discuss some methodological issues involved in this study.

A large part of the book is concerned with intensional contexts and with contexts involving the so-called "intentional idiom." These contexts include those constructed on what Russell calls verbs of "propositional attitude"—'believes that', 'knows that', 'hopes that', 'wishes that', etc. Another class of verbs belonging to the intentional idiom differs from these in not demanding to be followed by 'that' and a full sentential complement; 'seeks', 'hunts', and 'worships' are examples. There are puzzles concerning each of these kinds of verbs. Russell presents this famous one involving a propositional attitude:

* Titles of works cited will be abbreviated throughout the text. Full titles and publication data will be found in the Bibliography.

George IV wished to know whether Scott was the author of *Waverley,* and, in fact, Scott was the author of *Waverley.* It seems to follow, by Leibniz's Law of the substitutivity of identity, that George IV wished to know whether Scott was Scott. But, as Russell remarks, an interest in the Law of Identity can hardly be attributed to the first gentleman of Europe. This situation is paradoxical because we have apparently derived a false conclusion from two true premises by use of a valid logical principle.

Here we have, in a special case, an example of the kind of *failure of substitutivity* that is characteristic of nonextensional contexts. Chapter 3 is devoted to a discussion of Frege's analysis of these. He calls them "*ungerade*" (indirect or oblique) contexts. In chapter 4 I present Russell's solution to his puzzle about George IV. At the present time, philosophical logicians make a great deal of use of the idea of possible worlds in providing an account of intensional contexts. My view, following Kripke and others, is that possible-worlds semantics does provide an adequate account of the subclass of oblique contexts that are built on alethic modalities but that the case is quite otherwise for propositional attitudes. Hintikka is the chief advocate of possible-worlds analysis of propositional attitudes. In chapter 5 I examine his views. I conclude that the approach advocated by Hintikka constrains a kind of idealization on the concepts of knowledge and belief that makes it unsuitable for our purposes. I think that we do better to stick with the classical theories.

Another problem about intensional contexts, besides this one of failure of substitutivity, concerns quantification. Consider here Quine's puzzle: Necessarily, nine is greater than seven. It would seem to follow that there is something such that it is necessarily greater than seven. But what is that object? Nine?—for necessarily nine is greater than seven. Then the number of planets too is necessarily greater than seven, for nine is the number of the planets. But it is false that the number of planets is *necessarily* greater than seven; that is only contingently so. Apparently it makes no sense to say that there is something necessarily greater than seven. Apparently it makes no sense to *quantify into* an intensional context. This is Quine's conclusion. In chapter 6 I examine his arguments and argue, in turn, that in both Frege's and Russell's theories of meaning there is a solution to Quine's problem of *quantifying in.*

Frege's Puzzle. It was Frege who first provided a clear account of identity as a relation between objects. It is a relation that holds only between an object and itself. How then can anything informative be conveyed by true statements of identity? If '*a* = *b*' is true, how can it *say* anything other than '*a* = *a*'? This is the puzzle with which Frege begins his essay "On Sense and Reference" (Frege, [SR]). Chapters 1 and 2 are devoted to a study of Frege's solution to this puzzle and to a comparative study of Russell's solution.

Meinong's Puzzle. Consider the statement, 'Pegasus does not exist.' If it is true, then there is no such thing as Pegasus; i.e., 'Pegasus' denotes nothing. But how, asks Russell, can a nonentity be the subject of a proposition? If 'Pegasus' names nothing, how can there be a difference in meaning between 'Pegasus does not exist' and 'Cerberus does not exist'? How can they be talking about *different* things when neither thing is anything? This puzzle has to do with the working of singular terms that denote things that do not exist. The puzzle, as here presented, involves a difficulty when vacuous singular terms occur in true statements of nonexistence. It might be put this way: If Pegasus really does not exist, how can 'Pegasus' mean anything? And unless 'Pegasus' does mean something, doesn't 'Pegasus does not exist' also mean nothing? If these questions seem difficult to answer, it is because they challenge the naïve theory of meaning that we acquire in acquiring the use of the word 'meaning'. They call for refinement of this naïve notion.

Vacuous names are featured in other puzzles than those involved with true negative existential assertions. Here the problem is: How can we *say* truly of a nonexistent object that it does not exist? But there are parallel problems for vacuous names when combined with the intentional idiom. It is true that Ponce de Leon sought for the fountain of youth and not for the philosopher's stone. But how can there be this difference when each of these things is nothing at all? Since the fountain of youth is nonexistent, how can it be the object of an intentional act? What is the semantical role of 'the fountain of youth' in the true assertion, 'Ponce de Leon sought for the fountain of youth'?

These are some of the puzzles and paradoxes that force us to abandon the naïve theory of meaning acquired along with our language. The sophisticated alternatives that have been proposed cannot, therefore, fail to strike us as counterintuitive at certain points. The completely intuitive theory is, after all, incoherent. Our position is presented in the concluding words of Russell's essay "On Denoting":

> Of the many other consequences of the view I have been advocating, I will say nothing. I will only beg the reader not to make up his mind against the view—as he might be tempted to do, on account of its apparently excessive complication—until he has attempted to construct a theory of his own on the subject of denotation. This attempt, I believe, will convince him that, whatever the true theory may be, it cannot have such simplicity as one might have expected beforehand.

Some of our puzzles involve us in antinomies in which inconsistent conclusions are derived by apparently valid reasoning from true premises. Other puzzles cannot be so sharply focused as these. They involve something more like the incoherence or confusion that arises when we attempt to explain the working of such concepts as identity, existence, intentionality, and so on. What is common to all of the paradoxes is that in them principles of our naïvely held ideas of meaning clash with each other in such ways as to produce puzzlement or incoherence. In the very process of acquiring our language we also inevitably acquire a kind of primitive theory about its working. After all, such words as 'proper name', 'definition', 'sense', 'denotation', and 'meaning' are not technical terms. They are words of ordinary nontechnical language, and the more or less imprecise ways in which they are interrelated in language constitute a kind of primitive and unsophisticated theory of language. In acquiring our language we acquire the theory. The puzzles and paradoxes wreck this naïve theory and call for its replacement by a new one, the product of sophisticated reflection rather than passive, unconscious acquisition. There are now several competing alternatives for us to choose among, but the best, most detailed, comprehensive, profound, sophisticated, and satisfying are the classical theories of meaning of Frege and Russell. That is why I have chosen them from among others to be the center of attention here. Thus this is not a purely historical investigation. It would have been if subsequent work had managed to replace these classical theories with better ones. Then such a study as this might have found its justification in the consideration that, although we know better now, it helps us to appreciate our present position to have an accurate historical account of the errors and mistakes of older views that have been abandoned for these better present-day accounts. That is not the case. There are not today better theories than those of Frege and Russell, and it is for this reason that these views still remain at the center of interest in the philosophy of language. This claim, of course, must be defended with detailed argument, and I undertake to do this in the present work. This calls for the critical accounts I give of some alternatives to the classical theories—accounts due to Mill, Searle, Kripke, Wittgenstein, Quine, and others. Each of these authors advocates views at variance with those of Frege or Russell (or both). When examining the alternatives, I always aim at a decision as to who is right and why. Of course, in some cases the views do not conflict. The new theories are compatible with the older ones and supplement them. When that is so, I also try to indicate exactly where the advances have been made. Of course, many advances have been made since Frege and Russell. I always aim to arrive at such decisions, but I do not always succeed. Frege's and Russell's theories of meaning are the center of attention in this study, and it would have been satisfying to have determined that one of them is clearly a better theory than the other; but that is a conclusion I do not reach. Of course, there is no reason *a priori* why two or more theories dealing with a common subject matter should not be equally good, adequate, or acceptable. As far as I can determine, that indeed is the situation here. Frege's and Russell's theories are different and yet equally adequate. That is not to say that either is entirely adequate—that would be to say that they leave no problem unresolved and present no internal difficulties of their own. That is not so, and I have tried to present a detailed account of what the shortcomings are.

My project involves the comparison, examination, evaluation, and testing of theories. How, in this area, do we go about refuting or confirming a theory? There is a naive conception according to which we have, on the one hand, one or several theories and, on the other, a body of facts. To confirm or refute a theory we simply compare the theory with the facts. The difficulty with this simple model is that it is based on the assumption that we have available to us for inspection a body of facts that are themselves totally uncontaminated, so to speak, by any theory. But how good is this assumption? If all of us acquire a naïve theory of language in the very process of accquiring our language, then how can we succeed in prizing the theory off the facts so as to view them in their pristine state? Consider this example: A very controversial doctrine of Frege's is his view that full declarative sentences denote truth-values. After expounding this doctrine, David Bell remarks, "All this, regrettably, tells us nothing as to the *truth* of the doctrine that sentences denote their truth-values." He adds that he thinks that Frege's doctrine is both "obscure" and "highly implausible," and he finds reasons to reject it (David Bell, [*FTJ*], p. 28).

Bell's attitude is frequently encountered in discussions of these issues. I refer to him as typical rather than as eccentric. Apparently Bell thinks that it is either true or false that sentences denote their truth-values, and he thinks that Frege has chosen the wrong alternative. Moreover, Frege has chosen a view that is "implausible." Apparently Bell thinks that the plausible view is that sentences do not denote at all, either their truth-values or anything else. My diagnosis of this situation is that what Bell takes to be the plausible view is merely the one expressed by his naïve use of the word 'denote'. How are we to ask whether or not sentences 'denote' their truth-values unless we already give some sense to that word? And what sense can it have except the sense that it has already got in our language? Doesn't the feeling of "implausibility" arise, then, just from a conflict between the use the word 'denote' has in Frege's theory and its ordinary use? It makes no sense here to talk about a pure fact of the matter—a fact entirely free of contamination by theory. But why should our naïve, unexamined, use of the word 'denote' in ordinary language be the standard of what is plausible and true in a theory of language? After all, our naïve theory is not a very good theory, as is evidenced by the existence of the paradoxes and antinomies that wreck it and before which it is impotent. Why shouldn't it be regarded as a *discovery* that sentences denote truth-values? It can't just be a discovery if, as I have suggested, what we have is a new use—a technical use—of 'denote', an ordinary word. The real question ought to be whether this is a fruitful and productive concept as it is employed in the theory—whether it explains the facts and resolves paradoxes, and whether it does this better than competing alternatives. But, here again, we have this nagging appeal to the facts. If facts are merely the creations of theories, is there no external standard by which to judge the adequacy (truth) of theories?

Of course these are very large questions, not to be dealt with adequately within the scope of a mere Introduction. All I hope to accomplish here is to produce some skepticism about the use of terms like 'truth' and 'plausibility', in the manner exemplified by Bell, in evaluating and criticizing theories in the area of our discussions. Of course, somehow or other we do manage to compare theories of meanings with each other and with the real world they are supposed to explain. Somehow or other theories are even refuted by facts, and what we take to be facts are sometimes refuted by theories, too. How this is done is illustrated and explained the long way, *ambulando,* by the whole of what follows. I don't even attempt to say in a short way what is done. Probably the best way to refute a theory is with a better theory anyway, and not with a "fact."

It may, nevertheless, be of use to provide a brief account of how I see the matter. In order to understand what, e.g., Frege means by his technical terms, such as "reference," "proper name," and so on, we have to examine both his explicit elucidations and the actual role these concepts play in his theory of meaning. But if the theory is to be of interest, the sense of the terms, in their technical use, cannot be totally divorced from the sense these words have for us independently of Frege's theory or anybody else's theory. Otherwise the theory would not be a theory of *proper names,* of *sense,* of *denotation,* etc., at all. It would be a theory of other matters that are referred to, unaccountably, by these same terms. Because the terms in their theoretical use do share at least part of their sense with these terms in their ordinary use, we are entitled to our intuitions as to when the theory is right and when it goes astray. But initial impressions cannot be the last word in these matters. If our theory is working well on other fronts—in meeting difficulties and resolving paradoxes—we should be prepared to abandon our intuitions locally at certain points and conclude that the "facts" lie. One reason for doing this might be simply that we don't have an alternative theory that does better. What we seek is a kind of "reflective equilibrium" (I take this expression from John Rawls, [*TJ*], pp. 48–51, though my use of the expression perhaps differs from his) in which we test theories by our intuitions and, at the same time, are willing to test our intuitions by our theories. The better the theory, the more of these intuitions are preserved; but we should be prepared to abandon *any* of them. Further, some intuitions are stronger than others; hence, the better the theory, the less it requires us to abandon the stronger rather than the weaker of them. My own intuition is rather weak on the issue as to whether or not (declarative) sentences denote truth-values, or propositions, or nothing at all. Hence, if the best theory we have requires one of these choices, I'll go along with that. At any rate, our linguistic "intuitions," as I shall use this term, are the beliefs, principles, insights, etc., that are embodied in the naïve theory of our language that is encapsulated in the ordinary use of such terms as 'sense', 'reference', 'meaning', 'grammatical', etc. There is, therefore, nothing sacrosanct about these intuitions, though of course they must be respected.

Frege is the founder of analytical philosophy because he is the first philosopher to make the theory of meaning (the philosophy of language) the main discipline of philosophy (Dummett, [*Frege*], p. 666). Frege's central philosophical interest was not, however, the philosophy of language but the philosophy of mathematics; and his main thesis in the philosophy of mathematics is the thesis of logicism: that mathematics is part of logic.

In order to demonstrate logicism, Frege finds it necessary first to undertake a thorough reform of the existing logic. This leads to his most important contribution to science—the discovery of modern (mathematical) logic. Frege's theory of meaning is part of this discovery. What Frege constructed in his Begriffsschrift is extensional, impredicative, second-order, predicate logic.* Frege's theory of meaning is presented mainly as the semantics of this system of logic. But not everything of importance that he had to say in the philosophy

---

* "*Begriffsschrift*" and "Begriffsschrift": the word in italic letters is the name of Frege's first book; I use the same word in roman type for the name of the system of logic created by him. There does not seem to be an agreed translation for it in use by commentators on Frege writing in English; both "ideography" and "concept-script" have been used. The word is a neologism in German, although it can be found in use prior to Frege by the German philosopher Trendelenburg, who perhaps exerted some influence on Frege.

of language belongs to his account of the semantics of the Begriffsschrift. For one thing, this logic is purely extensional. Since his main concern is to establish the logicist thesis, he is able to limit his formal language to purely extensional contexts. As far as the aims of the philosophy of mathematics are concerned, he could have confined all his semantical theories to the purely extensional part of language. But this leaves nonextensional (intensional) contexts aside for special treatment, and Frege realizes the necessity that he give some indication of how his theory of meaning can be extended to deal with them. For one thing, it is only in virtue of this account of nonextensional contexts that one can justify the decision to exclude them from the Begriffsschrift—to set them aside for special treatment. Apart from such justification, the semantical theory underlying the Begriffsschrift would seem to be plagued by counterexamples to its principles on such a massive scale as to render it unacceptable. So Frege has to justify a special treatment of nonextensional contexts in order to defend the principles underlying his theory of meaning for the extensional part of language needed in the formalization of mathematics and the new logic. Since his main interest in intensional contexts is to show that his theory of meaning is not threatened by counterexamples, he does not need to provide a detailed treatment of these contexts; he needs only to give a rough indication of the general lines upon which he can deal with them. The details are, in fact, never supplied by Frege. He is content to indicate only the general outline of his theory of intensional contexts and to carry it far enough to convince himself and his critics that these contexts pose no threat to his extensional logic.

There is nothing inevitable about the decision to reserve intensional contexts for special treatment. Russell does not do so. Russell's and Whitehead's *Principia Mathematica,* like Frege's earlier work, aims to establish a philosophical thesis about the nature of mathematics, but its formulation of the language of mathematics is given within a larger framework, which includes intensional contexts. Here we note a radical difference between Frege's and Russell's theories of meaning.

Frege, then, is the originator of both modern logic and the philosophy of language in its modern form. He is consequently, as already noted, the originator of analytical philosophy—that kind of philosophy that deals with philosophical problems by translating them into problems in the theory of meaning and that deals with these problems with considerations derived from the theory of meaning. Frege's work in the theory of meaning originates as a by-product of his concern with the philosophy of mathematics. He does not develop the subject for its own sake until later in his career. He advances the doctrine that philosophical problems are problems about language not by explicit pronouncement and argument but by the example of his philosophical work. Both Frege and Russell regard natural languages as inadequate instruments for the formulation and solution of philosophical problems. They both think natural languages contain defects that, if unnoticed, can lead to philosophical error. Consequently, both undertake the construction of idealized, formal languages that avoid these defects, and they develop their theories of meaning in order to apply them, in the first place, to their alternative versions of an ideal language.

Given their great distrust for natural language and their avoidance of it in the development and defense of their theories of meaning, it may seem paradoxical to regard Frege and Russell as presenting philosophies of language at all. In this respect they are the founders of a tradition in the philosophy of language that includes nearly all of the main subsequent contributors to the subject. This tradition, starting with Frege, includes Russell, the early Wittgenstein, Carnap, Church, Tarski, and Quine. Each develops his contributions to the theory of meaning with reference, in the first place, to a formalized language and, more specifically, to the language of the first- or higher-order predicate calculus introduced by Frege. The work of these authors in the Fregean tradition nevertheless belongs to the philosophy of *language* in virtue of the assumption, which they share, that the underlying form of our language is that of predicate logic. The assumption is that, for example, in providing an account of singular reference, predication, truth, quantification, and atomic and compound statements in the formal language of predicate logic, the essential underlying mechanisms by which these devices and concepts operate in natural language are also revealed. The formal language and its semantical theory do not provide a naturalistic description of our language in its actual working but rather an idealized model of it. In providing an idealized model, abstraction is made from certain features of actual language, such as ambiguity and vagueness, that are not regarded as essential to the working of language, just as, in providing a scientific mechanics, abstraction is made from such features of the real world as the effect of friction in the air and bumps on the surface of planes along which real bodies descend. Of course, it is a theoretical decision that certain features of the actual situation can safely be ignored. No one, I suppose, would criticize the science of mechanics for ignoring friction, for formulating theories in terms of perfectly rigid bodies, and so on, but can we really justify such idealizing assumptions, in the theory of meaning, as the assumption that every proposition is either true or false and that there are no vague predicates such that it is not objectively the case that, for every object, either the predicate is true of it or false? Couldn't it be claimed that, in abstracting from vagueness for the purposes of theory construction, we have abstracted away not an accidental feature of language but part of its very essence? Indeed, it seems to me that much of the criticism of the classical theories of Frege and Russell does take this form. It criticizes the idealized models provided by these theories for lack of realism.

There is no general response to such criticism. The way to make it really effective is to provide another theory that is more realistic, i.e., that takes seriously some feature of actual language from which abstraction has been made in the work being criticized. If the new theory is otherwise as adequate as the older theories, it is obviously to be preferred on the ground of greater comprehensiveness and realism.

Nevertheless, all theories must abstract from some features of actual language, and this has methodological implications for the kinds of criticisms that can be made against them. One can't object to the principles of scientific mechanics by observing that no actual medium in which bodies fall is totally free of friction. Yet many criticisms that Saul Kripke, for example, brings against the theory of names in "the classical logical tradition" are of just this kind. For example, against Frege's view that ordinary proper names express a sense (or, on Russell's view, are to be treated as truncated forms of definite descriptions) Kripke makes this objection: "Common men who clearly use 'Cicero' as a name for Cicero may be able to give no better answer to 'Who was Cicero?' than 'a famous Roman orator', and they probably would say the same (if anything!) for 'Tully'. (Actually, most people probably have never heard the name 'Tully')" (Kripke, [PAB], p. 246). Now, it is very difficult for me to understand why Kripke should think such considerations are at all relevant to the question whether, in the theory of names, they are to be treated as having a sense that determines their reference. Citing an ordinary speaker's inability to come up with a definite description that expresses the sense of 'Cicero' as an objection to Russell's or Frege's theory is exactly on a plane with observing the existence of friction and taking its presence to be a refutation of scientific mechanics. Of course, the theories of Frege and Russell, though presenting idealized models of actual language, are meant to be theories capable of explaining certain features of actual language. In the terminology of recent linguistics, they are meant to have "psychological reality," to provide a "theory of competence" but not a "theory of performance." Actual linguistic practice is ultimately relevant in considering the acceptability of theories, but it is not relevant in the simple way in which Kripke supposes it to be in the passage quoted above and in many like passages in his critique of the theories of Frege and Russell.

The advocates of the "New Theory of Reference" share this rejection of Frege's concept of sense. Their task is to construct a better theory, and they have done serious and interesting work toward this end. These authors include Kripke, Donnellan, Putnam, and Burge, among others. It is obvious that a work defending the theories of Russell and Frege must deal with them. I have devoted the whole of chapter 7 to a discussion of some of Kripke's views. An important part of his contributions to logic is in the field of modal logic—the quantified logic of necessity and possibility. His theory of names, presented in his "Naming and Necessity", is given informally, but it is clear that it lends itself to a precise formulation in application to a formal language of quantified modality. To that extent, and in this way, Kripke too belongs to the Fregean tradition in the philosophy of language—in spite of his disclaimer that he doesn't want to provide an alternative theory at all but only a better "picture."

Neither Frege nor Russell was an advocate of modal logic, so a direct comparison of their theories with those of Kripke cannot be made. In order to carry through the comparison in spite of this, it is first necessary to develop natural extensions of the views of Russell and Frege so as to apply them to modal contexts. I do this, and the conclusion of my study of Kripke's theories is that a suitably modified version of Russell's theory of ordinary proper names—the description theory of proper names—survives Kripke's critique even if modal contexts are considered. Kripke also believes that he himself has refuted Frege's account of ordinary proper names. In fact, he does not really distinguish between the two classical views, for he calls them the "Frege-Russell theory." My conclusion about this is that, once we properly distinguish between Frege's theory and Russell's, we will find that Frege's view is not refuted by Kripke but is compatible with Kripke's theory. Kripke's arguments do undermine certain formulations of Russell's views about proper names—formulations that, it must be admitted, are supported by many of Russell's own discussions. Nevertheless, it is my view that a suitably cautious and careful formulation of a description theory of ordinary proper names—one that is certainly Russellian in spirit and that survives Kripke's critique—can be produced.

Oblique Contexts

1

Frege's Paradox about Identity

Frege's essay "On Sense and Reference" begins with his puzzle about identity. Is it a relation between objects or a relation between names? The statement 'Venus is the Morning Star' records important astronomical information. It must, then, be about that heavenly body and not about the alternative designations for the planet that are used in the statement. If this is so, then *identity* must itself be a relation between objects. A true statement of identity can assert of an object only that it has this relation to itself. But this is known to us *a priori;* it is an analytic truth. How then can a true statement of identity express an important advance in our knowledge or record an empirical discovery? Frege's puzzle is this: Since every true statement of identity says of an object that it stands in this relation to itself, how can there be any difference in cognitive value between trivial statements of identity, such as 'Venus is Venus', and informative statements of identity, such as 'Venus is the Morning Star'? A presupposition of this puzzle is that a statement of identity *can* express an important advance in our knowledge.

Frege's puzzle induces a related puzzle about any other relational statement. 'The number of planets is greater than seven' expresses astronomical information. The relation *greater than* is a relation between objects, and our statement is true just in case the object denoted by 'The number of planets' stands in this relation to the object denoted by 'seven'. But the object denoted by 'The number of planets' is the number nine, so our statement is true just in case 'Nine is greater than seven' is true. This, however, is trivial and known *a priori*. How then can there be a difference in cognitive value between the two? How can 'The number of planets is greater than seven' tell us anything other than 'Nine is greater than seven', since nine is the number of planets? Yet the two statements do convey entirely different information. Frege's puzzle is a puzzle about identity, but it is also a puzzle about any other relation. It arises as soon as we attempt to account for the cognitive content of a statement solely in terms of the objects denoted by the words we use in making it. The problem arises because we denote the same object with different names and thus construct different statements about the same object. A statement says something about the objects named in it. A mere change of names for the same thing cannot change the truth-value of what is said, but it can result in a vast change in its cognitive value.

The data for our puzzle are, then, these: the truth of an identity-statement requires that its singular terms denote the same object. The informativeness of an identity-statement requires that different names flank the identity-sign. Somehow, therefore, the difference between a trivial and an informative statement of identity must be explicable in terms of the differences in the names they use. Now a possible solution to the puzzle emerges. Can it be that what we learn is that the same object is denoted by different names and that this is what an informative statement of identity *says?* In that case, identity is, after all, *not* a relation between objects but a relation between names.

In his first book, *Begriffsschrift* (1879), Frege comes close to adopting this solution to his puzzle, and this leads him to a mistaken account of identity.

In *Begriffsschrift* Frege says, "Identity of content differs from conditionality and negation in that it applies to names and not to contents. Whereas in other contexts signs are merely representative of their content, so that every combination into which they enter expresses only a relation between their respective contents, they suddenly display their own selves when they are combined by means of the sign of identity of content; for it expresses the circumstance that two names have the same content" (Frege, [*FFG*], p. 20). Thus the introduction of the sign of identity into the Begriffsschrift has the consequence that all terms acquire a double meaning: "they stand at times for their content, at times for themselves" (Frege, ibid., p. 21).

Frege now goes on to give a geometrical example to show why the sign of identity of content is needed—how statements of identity can be informative.

Let a fixed point A lie on the circumference of a circle, and let a straight line rotate around this. When this straight line forms a diameter, let us call the opposite end to A the point B, corresponding to this position. Then let us go on to call the point of intersection of the straight line and the circumference the point B, corresponding to the position of the straight line at any given time; this point is given by the rule that to continuous changes in the position of the straight line there must always correspond continuous changes in the position of B. Thus the name B has an indeterminate meaning until the corresponding position of the straight line is given. We may now ask: What point corresponds to the position of the straight line in which it is perpendicular to the diameter? The answer will be: The point A. The name B thus has in this case the same content as the name A; and yet we could not antecedently use just one name, for only the answer to the question justified our doing so. The same point is determined in a double way:

(1) It is directly given in experience;
(2) It is given as the point *B* corresponding to the straight line's being perpendicular to the diameter.

To each of these two ways of determining it there answers a separate name. [Frege, [*TPWGF*], p. 11. The diagram is not Frege's; it was added by Peter Geach, the translator.]

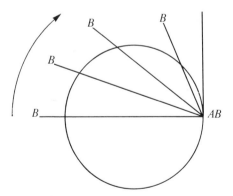

As the line turns clockwise, B moves until it coincides with A.

5

Note that Frege's early solution to his puzzle is essentially the same as that given in "On Sense and Reference," published thirteen years later, and the geometrical example from the *Begriffsschrift* is very like the one used in the later essay. What Frege means by "content" here is what he later calls "reference" (*Bedeutung*). He says, "One point is determined in two ways," and these different "ways of determining the same content" are just what he will later call the "sense" of the names.

Frege, then, already in his first publication on the subject, has his solution to his puzzle about identity. He says, ". . . the existence of different names for the same content is not always merely an irrelevant question of form; rather, that there are such names is the very heart of the matter if each is associated with a different way of determining the content. In that case the judgment that has the identity of content as its object is synthetic, in the Kantian sense" (Frege, [*FFG*], p. 21). Frege is saying that in a synthetic statement of identity we have sameness of content (and therefore truth) combined with different ways of determining that content. It is this latter feature that makes our statement not analytic like '$A = A$'. Yet, in this early work, Frege combines these insights with a mistaken account of identity.

Frege's *Begriffsschrift* combines his later solution to his puzzle with a mistaken view about the relation of identity. Russell, as we will see, has a correct understanding of identity, but he rejects Frege's solution to his puzzle. It is wrong, therefore, to suppose that we can't have a correct view of identity and reject the sense/reference distinction, and it is equally wrong to suppose that if we do recognize the distinction we can't have a wrong view about the nature of identity. These are separate issues.

Frege's mistake here is this. He sees that in a synthetic identity-statement the same "content" is determined in different ways. He concludes from this that what these statements say is that their names determine the same content. "Now let $\vdash (A \equiv B)$ mean that *the sign* A *and the sign* B *have the same conceptual content, so that we can everywhere put* B *for* A *and conversely.*" The same mistake occurs in the following argument: 'Socrates is a Greek' is true if, and only if, the denotation of 'Socrates' falls under the concept denoted by 'x is a Greek'. Therefore, 'Socrates is a Greek' just says that the denotation of 'Socrates' falls under the denotation of 'x is a Greek'.

In "On Sense and Reference" Frege tells why he abandoned his early view: "Nobody can be forbidden to use any arbitrarily producible event or object as a sign for something. In that case the sentence $a = b$ would no longer refer to the subject matter, but only to its mode of designation; we would express no proper knowledge by its means" (Frege, [SR], p. 57). I think that Frege here is alluding to the same considerations as those involved in the so-called "Church-Langford translation test" (Church, [CASAB]). Consider the statement

    (1)   Venus is the Morning Star.

According to the *Begriffsschrift* theory, which Frege now rejects, (1) says the same as

    (2)   'Venus' and 'the Morning Star' denote the same thing
          (in English).

If this supposition is correct, the translations of these two sentences into Italian must also convey the same information; that is,

    (1')   *Venere è la Stella Mattutina.*

must convey the same information as

    (2')   *'Venus' e 'the Morning Star' significano la stessa cosa*
          (in Inglese).

In translating (2) into (2'), it is necessary to leave the quoted material intact, for it is the names 'Venus' and 'the Morning Star' that are said to denote the same thing (in English). Any translation of (2) must be about these very names and not about their Italian translations, 'Venere' and 'la Stella Mattutina'. Suppose now that you are an Italian who does not understand any English at all. Then it is clear that (1') and (2') convey different information to you. (1') tells you an important astronomical fact, but (2') tells you nothing about the heavens at all. It tells you, rather, a fact about the English language. It is clear that (1') and (2') have different cognitive content. Then (1) and (2) must also convey entirely different information, and for the

7

same reason. (1) is about the heavens and (2) is about English words. Thus Frege is forced to abandon his earlier view.

This argument is rejected by both Quine and Dummett. Quine rejects it because it employs the unacceptable (to him) concept of synonymy. Dummett's reason is this:

> There is no ground for presumption that the practical canons of apt translation always require strict synonymy. On the contrary, translations of fiction and, equally, of historical narrative (including the Gospels) always translate even directly quoted dialogue; and, when a remark about a quoted word or phrase does not retain its truth-value under translation of the quoted expression, it is often regarded as allowable to substitute a non-equivalent expression for the one quoted. [Dummett, [*Frege*], p. 372]

Quine is right in thinking that our argument makes essential use of the concept of synonymy. If that concept is unacceptable, so is our argument; but if synonymy is an unintelligible notion, Frege's puzzle about identity is an unintelligible puzzle. It does not require a solution. Dummett, however, is mistaken in thinking that the argument depends on "practical canons of apt translation." To see this, let us adopt *his* canon and translate the quoted material in (2) while making the adjustment in the language referred to in that statement so as to conserve its truth.

(2'')   '*Venere*' e '*la Stella Mattutina*' *significano la stessa cosa (in Italiano)*.

We cannot maintain that (1') and (2'') have the same sense because, since (1) and (1') certainly are identical in sense, it would then follow that (1) and (2'') convey the same information, and certainly they do not. The argument turns on the concept of *sense* and not on rival conventions of translation. Dummett has missed Church's point. Neither (2') nor (2'') preserves the sense of (1').

Another argument against the metalinguistic interpretation of identity-statements contained in the *Begriffsschrift* is that it is impossible, on this conception, to provide a coherent account of the sense of statements such as $(x)(\exists y)(x = y)$, which combine identity and bound variables (Dummett, [*Frege*], p. 544).

The idea that a statement of identity is a statement about its singular terms evidently exerts a great attraction. Russell argues against it as follows:

> It might be suggested that "Scott is the author of Waverley" asserts that "Scott" and "the author of Waverley" are two names for the same object. But a little reflection will show that this would be a mistake. For if that were the meaning of "Scott is the author of Waverley," what would be required for its truth would be that Scott should have been *called* the author of Waverley: if he had been so called, the proposition would be true, even if some one else had written Waverley; while if no one called him so, the proposition would be false, even if he had written Waverley. But in fact he was the author of Waverley at a time when no one called him so, and he would not have been the author if everyone had called him so but some one else had written Waverley. Thus the proposition "Scott is the author of Waverley" is not a proposition about names, like "Napoleon is Bonaparte"; and this illustrates the sense in which "the author of Waverley" differs from a true proper name. [Whitehead and Russell, [*PM*], vol. 1, p. 67]

I detect here, I think, some wavering on Russell's part. 'Scott is the author of *Waverley*' is not a proposition about names, but 'Napoleon is Bonaparte' *is* a proposition about names. Russell does not say what proposition about names it is, but I assume it must be the proposition that 'Napoleon' and 'Bonaparte' are names for the same thing.

In "On Sense and Reference" (1892) Frege abandons his inadequate earlier theory of identity and presents his first and fullest account of the theory of sense and reference. He introduces the distinction in order to resolve his puzzle. Now he says: "A difference can arise only if the difference between the signs corresponds to a difference in the mode of presentation of that which is designated" ([SR], p. 57). He then gives this example:

Let *a, b, c*, be the lines connecting the vertices of a triangle with the midpoints of the opposite sides. The point of intersection of *a* and *b* is then the same as the point of intersection of *b* and *c*. So we have different designations for the same point, and these names ('point of intersection of *a* and *b*', 'point of intersection of *b* and *c*') likewise indicate the mode of presentation; and hence the statement contains actual knowledge.

The names 'the point of intersection of *a* and *b*' and 'the point of intersection of *b* and *c*' agree in reference (*Bedeutung*) but differ in sense (*Sinn*), "wherein the mode of presentation is contained." Going by the examples here and elsewhere, the sense or "mode of presentation" associated with a name is evidently a *criterion of identification* for the object denoted by the name. One and the same object can be identified according to different criteria, e.g., Venus may be recognized both as the Morning Star and as the Evening Star. The name *expresses* its sense and *denotes* its reference. The reference of a name is the object identified by the sense that the name expresses. Hence, sense is a *cognitive* concept. It is what we know when we understand a sentence or a name. What we know, in the case of a (declarative) sentence, is a criterion of identification of its truth-value, just as what we know when we understand any other name is a criterion of identification of its reference. In the notion of sense are combined both the notion of knowledge and the notion of identification. Thus this concept is fitted to resolve Frege's puzzle about the cognitive value of statements of identity. Think of the sense of a name as a *route* to its reference. One who understands the name (grasps its sense) has a route, or instruction, for recovering the reference of the name. Different routes may lead to the same place, and some are more direct than others. The sense of 'Venus' is the most direct criterion of identification of that planet; by comparison, the sense of 'the planet whose orbit is nearest to that of the earth' is a more indirect criterion for identifying that same object. It increases our knowledge to discover that two routes with which we are familiar actually terminate at the *same* place. Thus it was an important scientific discovery that the Morning Star and the Evening Star are the same planet. Because the concept of sense is a cognitive concept, if the senses of two names are the same, and one knows the senses of these names, one cannot fail to know that these senses *are* the same. But one can know the senses of two names for the same object without knowing that they are names for the *same* object. One cannot intelligibly ask, 'Is Venus the Morning Star?' unless one already knows the sense of 'Venus' and 'the Morning Star', but one may ask this question without knowing that these senses are alternative modes of presentation of the same object. Thus Frege solves his problem as to how true statements of identity can convey new information. He can now assert, without paradox, that identity is a relation that holds between objects.

In introducing the sense/reference distinction, one naturally appeals first to definite descriptions as illustrative examples, for they have a syntactic structure that exactly mirrors their semantic complexity. But Frege meant the distinction to apply to all logically relevant syntactic parts of complete sentences, including the sentence itself, as well as ordinary proper names, which lack logically relevant syntactic structure altogether. It is not hard to see why the reverse procedure—introducing the sense/reference distinction by starting with ordinary proper names as illustrative examples—is not the natural order. Indeed, such a procedure is rendered nearly unworkable by the paucity of relevant examples of ordinary proper names that agree in reference and differ in sense. And, scarce as these cases are, examples of ordinary proper names in the same language that *agree in sense* are even rarer. These are facts to be explained, but Frege's intention is clear. In a letter to P. E. B. Jourdain (undated) he give the following hypothetical example, which is very like one later made famous by Quine:

> Let us suppose that an explorer travelling in an unexplored country sees a high snow-capped mountain on the northern horizon. By making inquiries among the natives he learns that

its name is 'Alpha'. By sighting it from different points he determines its position as exactly as possible, enters it in a map. . . . Another explorer sees a snow-capped mountain on the southern horizon and learns that it is called 'Ateb'. . . . Later comparison shows that both explorers saw the same mountain. . . . What is stated in the proposition 'Ateb is Alpha' is certainly not the same thing as the content of the proposition 'Ateb is Ateb'. . . . I say, accordingly, that the sense of the name 'Ateb' is different from the sense of the name 'Alpha'. [Frege, [*PMC*], p. 80]

Frege then goes on to identify the sense of a name with the way its reference is determined. "An object can be determined in different ways, and every one of these ways of determining it can give rise to a special name, and these different names then have different senses; for it is not self-evident that it is the same object which is being determined in different ways" (ibid.). It is interesting that Frege does not give even a hypothetical example of two names with the *same* sense. Indeed, I do not think that many can be found if we insist on confining ourselves to a single language. But, if this restriction is removed, there is an abundance: 'London' and 'Londra' (in Italian), for example. Notice that, although he here writes explicitly about the sense of ordinary proper names, Frege does not identify the sense of a name with that of any definite description. If he had held the view that the sense of a name *is* that of some associated definite description, it would have been most natural for him to say so in connection with the example presented in this letter to Jourdain. Frege's theory is *not* the description theory.

2

Russell's Solution to Frege's Paradox

Russell rejected Frege's distinction between sense and reference. Indeed, he believed it to be incoherent (Russell, [OD], pp. 45–47). He was, of course, fully aware of the puzzle about identity that led Frege to draw the distinction, and he presented his own solution to the puzzle in accordance with the principle that the semantically relevant parts of sentences have denotation only and not sense. From a Fregean point of view, Russell collapses sense into reference; the sense of an expression is taken to be what it denotes.

It is difficult to appreciate the force of Russell's arguments unless we understand what his concept of a proposition was at the time. To do so, we begin with the notion of a *term* as it is used in Russell's *Principles of Mathematics*. According to Russell, the word "term" is "the widest word in the philosophical vocabulary." Anything we can think or talk about is a term, hence "to deny that such and such a thing is a term must always be false" (Russell, [*PoM*], p. 43). Russell's examples of terms include a man, a moment, a relation, a chimera, and the Homeric gods (ibid.). Of course, not all terms *exist;* some only subsist (a chimera, for example); but all terms have *being* in some sense. Notice that terms are *not* the words we use for talking about these things; they are the supposed things themselves. It follows that all expressions that grammatically are substantives stand for terms—for something whose being cannot be denied. In "On Denoting," Russell abandons part of the extreme realism of this earlier view, but the idea of expressions that necessarily stand for something whose being cannot be denied is retained in the concept of the logically proper name.

Just as words combine to form sentences, so the terms referred to by the logically relevant parts of sentences combine to form Russellian *propositions*. Thus propositions are not linguistic, but neither are they, as with Frege, abstract entities belonging to a "third realm." They are curious hybrids that are *complexes* of abstract and concrete entities. A general rule in reading Russell at this period is to remember that he is rarely interested in words for their own sake. He hurries past them to what they stand for, which is what is really relevant for logic. "*Words* all have meaning, in the simple sense that they are symbols which stand for something other than themselves. But a proposition, unless it happens to be linguistic [i.e., about words], does not itself contain words: it contains the entities indicated by words. Thus meaning, in the sense in which words have meaning, is irrelevant to logic" (Russell, [*PoM*], p. 47).

On this view, when we say, for example, 'Socrates is wise', the proposition that these words stand for ("indicate") actually contains Socrates, the man himself, as a constituent. In general, the terms that are the subject matter of *singular propositions* are among the constituents of these propositions. The contribution of a name to a proposition is the thing named. Predicates and expressions for relations also contribute components to propositions. In the sentence 'Socrates is wise' the name 'Socrates' contributes Socrates, and the expression 'is wise' contributes the attribute *wisdom* to the proposition that Socrates is wise. The proposition is a complex of these terms combined in an ultimate and indefinable way. On this view, a true sentence of the form '$A = B$' stands for a proposition whose constituent is A (i.e., B) and whose component is the identity-relation. Now if the sentence '$A = B$' is true, it follows that the sentence '$A = A$' stands for the same proposition, i.e., a proposition whose constituent is A and whose component is the identity-relation. Hence we have a "proof" of Frege's puzzle. Russell has transformed Frege's puzzle into a semantic principle: *There can be no true identity-propositions that are also informative.*

This account of singular propositions leads to a straightforward account of what it is for such propositions to be *about* a term: the relevant term is itself a constituent of the proposition. Propositions are structured entities. They may be represented as ordered *n*-tuples of their constituents and components. Consider, for example, the sentence 'Venus is the Morning Star'. The proposition it "indicates" is a structured entity that may be thought of as an ordered triple represented by the diagram

$$\langle O, \approx, O \rangle,$$

in which '*O*' represents the planet Venus and '$\approx$' represents the identity-relation. Since it is true that Venus is the Morning Star, the planet holds two positions in the proposition. Now compare this proposition with the one indicated by the sentence 'Venus is Venus'. This proposition is the same structured entity as the one represented above, assuming that indeed Venus *is* the Morning Star. Since the two sentences indicate the same proposition, they cannot differ in cognitive value. All true identity-propositions are trivial and uninformative. It would never be an advance in our knowledge to learn that an identity-proposition is true because we must already know that as soon as we understand any sentence denoting that proposition. We cannot understand a sentence of the form '$A = B$' unless we know the meanings of its parts, '*A*', '*B*' and '='. To know the meaning of these words is, for Russell, to be acquainted with what they denote. He formulated this in the principle that ". . . in every proposition that we can apprehend . . . all the constituents are really entities with which we have immediate acquaintance" (Russell, [OD], p. 56). If we are "acquainted" with *A* and with *B* and if *A* and *B* are the same thing, Russell assumes that we must know that they are the same. Hence the consequence that '$A = B$' can never be informative, if true.

(Perhaps a *caveat* is in order here. Russell, during the course of his long career, held many different views about the nature of propositions—and about many other subjects. What I have done, in presenting his views, is to pick out one line of thought that I find in his writing. No doubt there are also things he has written, at other times, that are inconsistent with what I here present as his views. Perhaps what I present as his views could best be described as the views I believe he sometimes held and that I think make the best sense of all of the things he says. My account may be considered as offered under the rubric *se non è vero, è ben trovato*. I am more concerned to present a *good* theory that can be seen as Russell's theory than in presenting one that is, historically, entirely accurate.)

Russell's solution to Frege's puzzle rests on his concept of logically proper names. A proper name (in the logical sense) is, for Russell, a name whose sense is its reference. Hence, as we have seen, if '*A*' and '*B*' are logically proper names for the same object, '*A* = *B*' stands for the same proposition as '*A* = *A*'. All statements constructed by placing the sign of identity between logically proper names are, if true, trivial and without cognitive value. In this way Russell proves that definite descriptions do not function logically as proper names. If 'the author of *Waverley*' were a logically proper name, then 'Scott is the author of *Waverley*' would, as we have seen, stand for the same proposition as 'Scott is Scott', provided that the former is true. But 'Scott is the author of *Waverley*' stands for a contingent and informative proposition, while 'Scott is Scott' stands for one that is necessary and trivial. Hence 'the author of *Waverley*' is not a logically proper name. Of course, identity-statements containing only what are ordinarily regarded as proper names do sometimes express valuable information—for example, 'Cicero is Tully'; and it was a discovery of some importance that Hesperus (the Morning Star) is Phosphorus (the Evening Star). From this Russell concludes that what are ordinarily called proper names are not logically proper names but disguised descriptions; such names function as descriptions, not as names.

Russell's view connects with an older tradition, the most well-known exponent of which was John Stuart Mill. Common names, for Mill, have both connotation and denotation. Thus 'horse' connotes certain properties, and the name 'horse' denotes the things that have those properties. By contrast, proper names have no connotation; they do not denote in virtue of the possession of certain properties by their denotations but, so to speak, directly. Thus Socrates received his name by being dubbed 'Socrates'; and he might just as well have been given any other name.

This contrast is misleading. After all, we might have named horses by another name, too; e.g., 'cow' or '*Pferd*'. However, once the convention by which they are called 'horses' is established, it is not correct to call them 'cows'. A horse is not a cow. Just so, Socrates could have been named 'Plato' or 'Moses', but, once he has been named 'Socrates', it is just as wrong to call him 'Plato' as it is to call a horse a 'cow'. What is correctly called a 'horse' is so called in virtue of its possession of certain properties, just as what is called 'Socrates' is so called in virtue of *his* possession of the requisite properties. From this point of view, proper names are words like any others. At any rate, Frege had no need to treat ordinary proper names as disguised descriptions because he held, against Mill, that all singular terms have sense (connotation) as well as reference (denotation). For Frege, what are ordinarily called proper names *really are* proper names. The relevant consideration about Mill's view for us is this: there seems to be no way for him to deal with Frege's puzzle about identity.

Russell's solution to Frege's puzzle is a consequence of his theory of definite descriptions. Every informative statement of identity must include in its surface grammar either an explicit description, an ordinary proper name such as 'Hesperus', which is a 'disguised' description, or an incomplete symbol of some other kind.

> The usefulness of *identity* is explained by the above theory. No one outside a logic-book ever wishes to say '*x* is *x*', and yet assertions of identity are often made in such forms as 'Scott was the author of *Waverley*' or 'thou art the man'. The meaning of such propositions cannot be stated without the notion of identity, although they are not simply statements that Scott is identical with another term, the author of *Waverley,* or that thou art identical with another term, the man. The shortest statement of 'Scott is the author of *Waverley*' seems to be 'Scott wrote *Waverley;* and it is always true of *y* that if *y* wrote *Waverley, y* is identical with Scott'. It is in this way that identity enters into 'Scott is the author of *Waverley*'; and it is owing to such uses that identity is worth affirming. [Russell, [OD], p. 55]

In this account, 'Scott is the author of *Waverley*' is not logically an identity-statement at all. Its true underlying logical form is displayed only after the definite description 'the author of *Waverley*' is eliminated in accordance with Russell's theory of descriptions. Since, according to this theory, there are no informative identity-statements, Frege's puzzle as to how there can be such rests on a false assumption, made because the surface grammar of these pseudo identity-statements is taken as a reliable indicator of their true logical form. Russell's solution to Frege's puzzle consists, then, in providing a theory according to which all instances of the puzzle (all apparently informative identity-statements) are to be systematically *eliminated*. Once all definite descriptions—and other kinds of incomplete symbols—are eliminated from the language, we eliminate, as well, all instances of purportedly informative identity-statements. (This way of interpreting Russell comes from George Bealer's unpublished "On Russell's Theory of Meaning.")

For Russell, apparently informative statements of identity always involve this disparity between superficial grammatical form and underlying logical form. For example, the surface grammatical form of 'Scott is the author of *Waverley*' is that of an identity-statement, $S = (\imath x)(Wx)$. But descriptions are incomplete symbols, and the underlying logical form of the latter statement is that of an existential generalization:

$$(\exists c)(x)[(Wx \equiv x = c) \cdot (c = S)].$$

It is characteristic of Russell's theory of meaning to distrust surface grammar and to seek the true logical form of statements beneath this disguise. This program is a reflection, in the theory of meaning, of Russell's ontological program of logical construction, conducted according to the principle: Wherever possible, replace inferences to unknown entities by logical constructions out of known entities. An incomplete symbol is the linguistic image of a logical construction. The concept of an object and the concept of a name are mutually dependent, so neither can be explained without reference to the other. An object is what is, or can be, denoted by a name—its objective correlative; and names are expressions that denote objects. The point is exemplified by Frege's procedure in *Grundlagen der Arithmetik*. In order to show that numbers are objects, he thinks it sufficient to show that numerals really do function logically as names; hence his emphasis on the importance of fixing the sense of numerical identities ("recognition judgments") concerning numbers. Conversely, to show that some purported objects are not really objects is to show that their purported names are, logically, not real names. Russell calls such names "incomplete symbols." The method of demonstrating that they are not really names is their contextual definition "in use." By effecting the elimination of the pseudo names from any context in which they occur, contextual definition at the same time accomplishes the "logical construction" of their purported objective correlatives. Frege's theory of meaning exhibits an opposed tendency. It is carried out according to the principle: Trust the surface grammar, wherever possible, as a reliable indicator of underlying logical form. The resulting Fregean theory of meaning is one in which, as much as possible, semantics mirrors surface grammar; semantical complexity mirrors syntactical complexity. For example, just as there are atomic syntactic units in the category of proper names, for Frege there are also senses of these syntactic atoms: atomic senses or individual concepts. A connected difference is in opposing attitudes toward contextual definition. Russell, of course, favors contextual definition as the principal means of carrying through his program of logical construction. Frege, on the other hand, opposes contextual definition as methodologically unsound. Russell's program leads to a maximization of the class of syncategorematic expressions in language, while Frege's program maximizes the class of categorematic expressions, the class of names.

Is there any reason to prefer Russell's solution to Frege's puzzle over Frege's own solution? An advantage for Russell's might be thought to be found in its dispensing with sense. Russell's theory is a purely denotational theory of meaning that attaches a single semantical value to each relevant expression, and it would seem therefore to have an advantage of simplicity in comparison with Frege's semantic dualism. The following diagrammatic representation of the two accounts shows the nature of the simplification that Russell's theory achieves. (These diagrams are patterned on those used by Terence Parsons in his article "Frege's Hierarchies of Indirect Senses and the Paradox of Analysis" [Parsons, [FHIS], pp. 41–42]. The prepositive form '$= A\ B$' is used instead the more familiar '$A = B$'.) The upward arrows represent the *expressing* relation: a name *expresses* its sense. The downward arrows represent the *denotating* relation. The broken arrows represent the relation the sense of a name has to the object the name denotes. It is the relation of *being a concept* of that object. (This accords with Church's use of this term. It is not Frege's use of "concept.") A name *denotes* that object of which its sense is a concept. In terms of the algebra of relations, for Frege the relation of denoting (D) is the relative product of the relation of

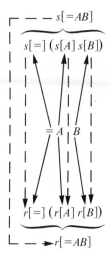

Fregean Semantics of '$A = B$'

expressing (E) into the relation of being a concept of an object (C); $D = E/C$. In this sense, the upper half of the diagram yields the lower half. '$s[D]$' means the sense of (the designator) 'D'; '$r[D]$' means the reference of (the designator) 'D'. The parentheses represent the application of function to argument, so that, e.g., the sense of '$A = B$' ($s[=AB]$) is got by applying the sense of '$=$' (which is a function) to the sense of 'A' and the sense of 'B' as arguments. The sense of '$A = B$' is a *thought*—a concept of the truth-value that is the denotation of the sentence '$A = B$'. For Frege, denoting is an *indirect* relation routed through sense. In the simple case of the isolated designator 'D' the picture of the route is given at the top of page 21. The corresponding diagram for the trivial statement '$A = A$' would differ, in the upper half, only in that, in place of '$s[B]$', our new diagram would have '$s[A]$'. This represents the *whole* difference in the senses of the two sentences.

By contrast, the diagram for the Russellian semantics of the same sentence is that shown on the lower left of page 21. Here 'A' denotes A, ($r[A]$); 'B' denotes B, ($r[B]$); and '$=$' denotes $=$, ($r[=]$). The constituents are combined by the component, by application of function to argument, into the structured entity represented as the ordered triple of these entities. This last is the proposition denoted

$s[D]$

D

$r[D]$

by '$A = B$'. The proposition that $A = B$, if true, is, as we have seen, the same as the proposition that $A = A$. The diagram for the isolated designator D is shown on the right below.

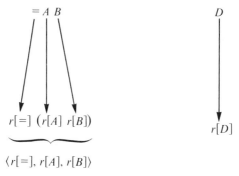

Russellian Semantics for '$A = B$'

Here reference is *direct;* the route through sense is eliminated. The simplification results in a theory that replaces Frege's three relations—*expressing, being a concept of an object,* and *denoting*— with one relation, *denoting;* and it replaces Frege's two entities— sense and reference—with one entity, reference.

The question that naturally arises now is this: What feature or features of Russell's theory allow for this great apparent simplification? What, so to speak, is the price paid for it? Does Frege's complexity really gain him nothing? The answer is that Russell pays the price by imposing an intensional interpretation on his logic from the beginning. Frege develops an extensional logic because he has the sense/reference distinction. Thus he is able to set aside intensional contexts for special treatment. Without that distinction, Russell's logic must be interpreted intensionally if the language of *Principia Mathematica* is to serve the purpose for which it was developed and if some of Russell's most important contributions are to be preserved.

For present purposes I propose to consider *Principia Mathematica* as a *language* that with the addition of primitive singular and predicate constants (amounting roughly to the entire *Who's Who* plus the *OED*) is potentially capable of expressing any matter of empirical fact or any mathematical or logical proposition.

Russell can't dispense with intensions without readmitting Frege's puzzle in somewhat altered form. In the case of full (declarative) sentences, Frege's puzzle is this: How can '$p = q$' differ in cognitive value from '$p = p$', provided the former is true? The discovery of the truth of a statement of the form '$p = q$' is sometimes an important advance in our knowledge, while '$p = p$' is trivial. The semantics of Frege's Begriffsschrift leaves no place for a distinction between '$p \equiv q$' and '$p = q$'. An example of an informative statement of the latter form would be one expressing the equivalence of the axiom of choice and the principle that every set can be well ordered. Since Frege employs the sense/reference distinction in all logical types of expressions, his solution for this form of the puzzle is the same as that already discussed. The sentences replacing 'p' and 'q' have the same truth-value, provided that '$p = q$' is true, but they express different thoughts, provided that '$p = q$' is informative. The two thoughts express alternative criteria of identification of the same truth-value.

How can Russell deal with this form of the puzzle? Russell's logic, unlike Frege's, does provide a distinction between '$p \equiv q$' and '$p = q$'; it is a distinction between the relation of equivalence and the relation of identity. This distinction can, however, be drawn only on an intensional interpretation of the logic. The values of the variables must be taken as propositions in the abstract sense, not as truth-values. Because the values of the variables 'p' and 'q' are taken as truth-values, in the Begriffsschrift account, there is no difference, on that account, between equivalence and identity; equivalent truth-values *are* identical. There *is* a distinction, however, between equivalent and identical propositions. For example, the axiom of choice is a different proposition, we may assume, from the well-ordering principle, since it was an important advance in our knowledge when they were proven to have the same truth-value.

A Russellian response then, to the present form of Frege's puzzle would be this: What are, for Frege, cases of informative identities of the form '$p = q$' are not identities at all but statements of equivalence between propositions; there can be no informative identities. This response is possible only on an intensional interpretation of Russell's logic. But having admitted *propositions* as the values of Russell's variables, we are committed to them as a new kind of entity and so cannot deny them access to the identity-relation. "No entity without identity." In fact, in *Principia*, Russell does recognize formulas of the form '$p = q$' as well formed (Whitehead and Russell, [*PM*], p. 659). It would seem that, once we have recognized propositions as *objects,* there is nothing to prevent our language from containing two names for the same proposition, say 'A' and 'B', such that '$A = B$' is an informative statement. Yet, on the intensional interpretation, it cannot be both informative and true. Is there a Russellian solution to this form of Frege's puzzle? (I intend only to raise this question here, and to postpone further discussion of it.)

Objection might be made here that we might have recourse to still another interpretation of the letters 'p', 'q', 'r', etc., of "propositional logic." This is Quine's interpretation, according to which they are not genuine variables at all, as they are for Frege and Russell, but schematic letters holding places for sentences. They are not variables because, for Quine, they are never to appear within quantifiers. The sentences that replace the letters are, consequently, not interpreted as *names* of objects that have access to the identity-relation. For Quine, '$p = q$' is not well formed, since '$=$' demands to be flanked by names; '$\equiv$' is not the name of a function but a syncategorematic connective that, applied to statements two at a time, produces another statement.

This interpretation of the letters '*p*', '*q*', '*r*', etc., of "propositional logic" is not open to Russell or Frege because they both *do* in fact allow propositional variables to appear in quantifiers. Russell is uneasy about this, as is indicated by this remark preceding the theorem *14.3: "In this proposition, however, the use of propositions as apparent variables involves an apparatus not required elsewhere, and we have not therefore used this proposition in subsequent proofs." Russell's uneasiness about bound propositional variables is not explained, but it goes along with his rejection of Frege's idea of sentences as names. "On grounds not connected with our present question, we cannot regard propositions as names . . ." (Whitehead and Russell, [*PM*], p. 659). This doctrine is, in turn, connected with Russell's desire to treat propositions as logical constructions and the sentences that denote them as incomplete symbols.

> It will be seen that, according to the above account, a judgment does not have a single object, namely the proposition, but has several interrelated objects. That is to say, the relation which constitutes judgment is not a relation of two terms, namely the judging mind and the proposition, but is a relation of several terms, namely the mind and what are called the constituents of the proposition. [Ibid., p. 43]

We have noted Russell's tendency to treat propositional variables as bindable and his tendency to treat propositions as logical constructions and to treat expressions for them (declarative sentences) as incomplete symbols. The two tendencies are incompatible. If propositional variables are bindable, then their substituends, declarative sentences, are names of objects, i.e., of propositions. I would urge that for present purposes it is best to reject the second of the two tendencies, i.e., to reject what Church calls the "fragmentation" of propositions involved in treating them as logical constructions. The reason is that bound propositional variables are needed in *Principia* if it is to serve the purpose of a *language* in which *any* factual statement can be formulated. The point is made by Church: ". . . there are many entirely ordinary assertions whose restatement in a Principia-like language would seem to require this [possibility of quantifying with respect to propositional variables]" (Church,

[margin handwritten note:] Not necessarily! Russell might — and should — give an account of propositional quantification in terms of quantification over relations (including properties). It's hard to see how to do this, but that doesn't show it's impossible.

24

[RSTT], p. 23). Consider, for example the statement '*a* is sometimes mistaken', which may be represented as

$$(\exists p) \cdot B^n \ (a,p) \cdot \sim p,$$

where '*B*' stands for 'believes' and the superscript '*n*' indicates the type restrictions on the propositions over which the bound variable ranges. '*a* is not omniscient' is

$$\sim (p) \cdot B^n \ (a,p) \equiv p.$$

'*a* believes everything asserted by Aristotle,' may be represented as

$$A^n \ (\alpha,p) \supset {}_p B^n \ (a,p).$$

Or consider the dictum of Petrus Ramus that all assertions of Aristotle are false,

$$A \ (\alpha,p) \supset {}_p \sim p.$$

If we assume that Aristotle rather than Petrus asserts this and that it is the only assertion he ever makes, we obtain an antinomy (Church, [RSTT], pp. 23–24). The superscript '*n*' indicates type restrictions required to remove this proposition from the range of its own quantifier in order to avoid the antinomy. Church proposes that in place of the two primitive predicates, '*B*' and '*A*', we introduce two infinite sequences of primitive predicates of orders 1, 2, 3, . . . , for each positive integer *n*. Then $A^n \ (x, p)$ and $B^n \ (x, p)$ are to be interpreted as false for any *x* for any value of *p* that involves assertions or beliefs of order $\geq n$. Hence each antinomy-producing assertion that Aristotle asserts, at each order *n*, of himself that all of his assertions, at order *n*, are false,

$$A^n \ [\alpha, A^n \ (\alpha,p) \supset {}_p \sim p],$$

is itself counted as false. It remains paradoxical that no assertion, true or false, can be made about all of Aristotle's assertions without restriction of order (Church, [RSTT], p. 24). Antinomies never come

25

with solutions that do not entail some paradoxical consequences of their own. (For further discussion about the use of infinitely many primitive predicates, see the last section of chapter 3.)

Thus the language of *Principia Mathematica* is best understood to contain bound propositional variables. Propositions, therefore, must be given access to the identity-relation, and the question arises whether this won't result in new forms of Frege's puzzle that cannot be eliminated, since there is nothing to prevent our language from containing alternative names for these objects and thus making informative identity-statements about them possible. It is not clear in all cases how the identities are to be eliminated.

Alonzo Church has raised a similar doubt about Russell's treatment of Frege's puzzle. In Russell's theory, definite descriptions of objects of lowest logical type (individuals) can all be eliminated. What appears in the analyzed form of the statements containing these descriptions, however, are names of properties. With respect to *these* names, instances of Frege's puzzle may appear all over again. How can '$A = B$' be informative and '$A = A$' not be if the former is true and 'A' and 'B' name a single property such as *being an author of Waverley?* Church's doubt is expressed as follows: "On a theory of the Russell type the difficulty arises that names of properties seem to be required, and on pain of readmitting Frege's puzzle about equality (which leads to the distinction of sense and denotation in connection with names of any kind), such names of properties either must be analyzed away by contextual definition—it is not clear how—or must be so severely restricted that two names of the same property cannot occur unless trivially synonymous" (Church, [NAESA], n. 14). This is not a problem for Frege, because the distinction between sense and reference is applicable to names of objects in all logical types, including names of properties.

When are two names names of the same property? When are two properties the same? Extensionally, properties are counted as the same if they belong to the same objects. If we identify properties with Frege's concepts, then the identity-condition that he adopts for properties is this: they are extensional. Strictly speaking, identity is not, for Frege, a relation that holds between concepts; it is a relation between *objects*. There is, however, an analogue of the relation of identity that does hold between concepts, namely coextensiveness.

Since concepts are incomplete entities, they should be designated by incomplete names—names with one or more Greek letters serving to hold places open for names of arguments to the functions denoted by these incomplete names. So, for Frege, the analogue to an identity-statement for concepts is of the form $(x)(Fx \equiv Gx)$. There is also an analogue for concepts to Frege's puzzle about identity of objects. The form of his puzzle for such statements is this: How can $(x)(Fx \equiv Gx)$ ever differ in cognitive value from $(x)(Fx \equiv Fx)$, provided the former is true? A Fregean answer is that the incomplete names 'Fx' and 'Gx' agree in reference; they denote the same concept if $(x)(Fx \equiv Gx)$ is true, but they differ in sense if the latter is informative.

There is an objection to coextensiveness as the criterion of identity for properties, or concepts, from Russell's point of view. It obliterates the only distinction there is between classes and properties. This objection does not apply to Frege's theory because, for him, there is still a difference between concepts and classes, even though both are extensional. Classes are objects, and concepts are functions. No function is an object. But for Russell there is *no* difference between properties, understood extensionally, and classes. Russell, however, needs this distinction in order to deal with Frege's puzzle in its class form. How can $\hat{x}(\phi x) = \hat{x}(\psi x)$ ever differ in cognitive value from $\hat{x}(\phi x) = \hat{x}(\phi x)$, provided the former is true? 'Creatures with a heart are creatures with a kidney' is informative, while 'Creatures with a heart are creatures with a heart' is not.

The Russellian solution to this form of Frege's puzzle is exactly the same as his solution to the form of the puzzle involving definite descriptions. Classes are regarded as logical constructions and their names—class abstracts—are incomplete symbols, just as are definite descriptions. Classes are not part of the ultimate logical furniture of the world. The contextual definition for class abstracts is given in *20.01, where $\phi\hat{x}$, $\psi\hat{x}$ are variables for propositional functions and $\phi!\hat{x}$, $\psi!\hat{x}$ are of lowest order:

$$*20.01 \quad f\{\hat{z}\,(\psi z)\}.=:(\exists\phi)\colon \phi!x. \equiv_x. \psi x : f\{\phi!\hat{z}\} \text{ Df.}$$

The informative identity $\hat{x}(\theta x) = \hat{x}(\psi x)$ is, in accordance with this definition, an abbreviation for:

$$(1) \quad (\exists \phi):. \ \phi!x. \ \equiv_x. \ \psi x :. (\exists \pi): \pi!x. \ \equiv_x. \ \theta x : \pi!\hat{x} = \phi!\hat{x}.$$

The trivial identity $\hat{x}(\theta x) = \hat{x}(\theta x)$, on the other hand, is an abbreviation of:

$$(2) \quad (\exists \phi) :. \ \phi!x. \ \equiv_x. \ \theta x :. (\exists \pi) : \pi!x. \ \equiv_x. \ \theta x : \pi!\hat{x} = \phi!\hat{x}.$$

Since (1) and (2) differ in cognitive value, we have thus solved Frege's puzzle in its class form. The solution depends on rejection of the extensional interpretation of properties in favor of an intensional interpretation. On the extensional interpretation, $\psi\hat{x}$ and $\theta\hat{x}$ are the same property, since by (1) they are coextensive with properties identical with each other. On this interpretation, (1) and (2) are the same in cognitive value; hence $\hat{x}(\theta x) = \hat{x}(\phi x)$, on this interpretation, does not differ in cognitive value from $\hat{x}(\theta x) = \hat{x}(\theta x)$.

In his Introduction to the first edition of *Principia Mathematica* (1910), Russell explicitly rejects the extensional interpretation of propositional functions:

. . . two functions may well be formally equivalent without being identical; for example,

$$x = \text{Scott.} \ \equiv_x. x = \text{the author of } \textit{Waverley},$$

but the function "$\hat{z} = $ the author of *Waverley*" has the property that George IV wished to know whether its value with the argument "Scott" was true, whereas the function "$\hat{z} = $ Scott" has no such property, and therefore the two functions are not identical. [Whitehead and Russell, [PM], pp. 83–84]

Now, however, we can raise the issue of Frege's puzzle once again, this time for propositional functions on the intensional interpretation. How can $\pi!\hat{x} = \phi\hat{x}$ differ in cognitive value from $\phi\hat{x} = \phi\hat{x}$, provided the former is true? We have considered three forms of Frege's puzzle: one involving definite descriptions, one involving full sentences, and one involving class abstracts. The Russellian solution turns on treating definite descriptions and class abstracts as incomplete symbols. Eliminating these incomplete symbols by contextual definition brings with it the elimination of all the instances of the appropriate forms of Frege's puzzle as well. But names of propositional functions, since they are paradigm cases of *complete* symbols, are not candidates for elimination.

Are we then left with a form of Frege's puzzle that can be dealt with in Frege's theory of meaning but not in a Russellian theory? I am not sure what the answer is to this question, but I make the following remarks on behalf of the Russellian. Russell could argue that it remains to be shown that there *are* any instances of Frege's puzzle for properties (concepts, propositional functions) on the intensional interpretation of these entities, to which Russell is committed. To be sure, there are well-formed formulas having the form $\phi\hat{x} = \psi\hat{x}$. But '$\phi\hat{x}$' and '$\psi\hat{x}$' are variables, not constants; so '$\phi\hat{x} = \psi\hat{x}$' is not a sentence, as required for a form of Frege's puzzle. An actual case of Frege's puzzle would be a true sentence of this form that was informative. Now it seems easy enough to find true sentences of this form, e.g., 'Being erotic is being sexy', 'Being succulent is being juicy'. The assumption is that the property of being sexy is identical with the property of being erotic; the property of being succulent is identical with the property of being juicy. But it is doubtful that 'Being erotic is being sexy' differs in cognitive value from 'Being sexy is being sexy' or that 'Being succulent is being juicy' conveys any information not conveyed by 'Being succulent is being succulent'. Could anyone know what it is to be sexy and know what it is to be erotic and not know that being sexy *is* being erotic? One can know what the Morning Star is and what the Evening Star is *without* knowing that they are the same. That is why 'The Morning Star is the Evening Star' is a genuine case of Frege's puzzle. But are there any cases of Frege's puzzle for properties that satisfy both the necessary conditions of being informative and being true? 'Being a creature with a heart is being a creature with a kidney' is not a true identity on the intensional interpretation, to which the Russellian is committed. In fact, informative identities are all false on this interpretation. Consequently, there can be no cases of Frege's puzzle for properties, and this is the Russellian solution. The same solution applies when the designators are full declarative sentences.

This discussion is unsatisfactory because it turns essentially on the notion of identity and difference for properties without providing a clear criterion of identity for them. Coextensionality is a clear criterion, but we have shown that it is unacceptable from Russell's, though not from Frege's, point of view. I have an intuition that the property of being a creature with a heart is not the same property as the property of being a creature with a kidney and that the property of being erotic is the same property as the property of being sexy. But I have no clear intuition of a true statement of identity for properties that is also nontrivial and informative. This is exactly as it should be from the Russellian point of view, according to which names of properties are logically genuine names. In Russell's view there cannot be any genuine identity-statements that are also informative.

The same kind of treatment may also suffice for the case of identities of the form '$p = q$'. If they are informative, the two sentences must stand for *different* propositions, and therefore the identity-statement itself will be false. It is interesting to compare the Russellian solution of this form of the puzzle with Frege's own solution. Frege allows informative identities of the form '$p = q$' and explains them by appeal to the difference of the propositions that the two sentences express. If this treatment is adequate, so must the Russellian account be adequate; for it takes these same propositions as the denotata of the sentences and thus as different if the original identity is informative. On Frege's account there are true statements of identity that are informative, and, on Russell's account, any informative statement of the form '$p = q$' will not be true. The difference in the propositions expressed, which guarantees the adequacy of the Fregean solution to this form of Frege's puzzle, therefore also guarantees the adequacy of the Russellian solution. The two accounts succeed or fail together at this point.

We have here a special case of a more general situation: Russellian solutions to intensional paradoxes can be mapped systematically onto Fregean solutions and conversely. These relations are represented in the diagram as shown on page 31.

If $p = q$ is both true and informative, then, as the Frege portion of the diagram illustrates, the senses of the sentences $s[p]$ and $s[q]$ are different concepts of the True. These "thoughts" are associated with their Russellian counterparts, $R[p]$ and $R[q]$, which, as is shown in the center portion of the Russell diagram, are different propositions, both true. On the Frege side, the semantic dualism (expressing and denoting) is represented by the contrasting arrows,

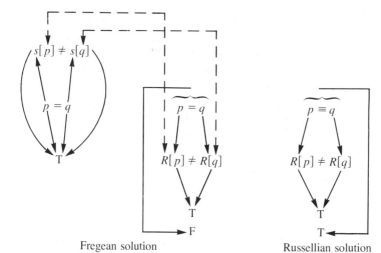

Fregean solution   Russellian solution

up and down. Russell's semantic monism dispenses with the entire upper half of the Frege diagram, but all of the latter's complexity is retained. The Russellian identity, of course, is *false* because the denoted propositions are different. Remember that Russell transforms Frege's paradox into the principle: *There are no informative identities that are also true.* The corresponding Russellian truth is the biconditional $p \equiv q$, and this is also informative. The transformations can be made in either direction, from the Frege side of the diagram to the Russell side or conversely; if there is a Fregean solution to this form of Frege's paradox about identity, there is a Russellian solution and conversely.

Alonzo Church says, "I believe that . . . there is now rather wide recognition that Russell's logic must be understood intensionally if some of its significant features are to be preserved" (Church, [RSTT], p. 22). In this interpretation the values of the propositional-functional variables are to be *properties* rather than classes for singulary functional variables and are to be generally *n*-ary *relations in intension* for *n*-ary functional variables. Similarly, the values of Russell's propositional variables must be taken as intensional, i.e., as propositions in the abstract sense rather than as truth-values. Consequently, sentences must be taken as names of propositions, since they are substitutable for propositional variables (Church, ibid.).

Russell wrote the Introduction to the second edition of *Principia Mathematica* (1925) under the strong influence of Wittgenstein's *Tractatus Logico-Philosophicus* and its rejection of the intensional point of view. In the second edition he acknowledges the arguments against the axiom of reducibility and proposes to replace it with axioms of extensionality for each type while preserving the ramified types. It is ironic that, under Wittgenstein's influence, Russell was thus led to advocate a course that would have obliterated some of his most important contributions to logic and the theory of meaning. But even while proposing to move in this direction, Russell expresses grave reservations about it. He says, of the axiom of reducibility, ". . . clearly it is not the sort of axiom with which we can rest content" ([ISE*PM*], p. xiv). He goes on to say that there is another course recommended by Wittgenstein the consequences of which he now intends to develop. Wittgenstein's course is "to assume that functions of propositions are always truth-functions, and that a function can only occur in a proposition through its values" (ibid.). The view involves the consequence that "all functions of functions are extensional" (ibid.). How this is possible, he says, "is shown in *Tractatus Logico-Philosophicus*" (ibid.). But he does express caution: "There are difficulties in the way of this view, but perhaps they are not insurmountable." He adds, finally, "We are not prepared to assert that this theory is certainly right, but it has seemed worthwhile to work out its consequences in the following pages" (ibid.). The most important consequence, from my point of view, is that the proposed extensional reformulation of Russell's logic makes a comparison between Russell's and Frege's theory of meaning a pointless and barren exercise.

On several occasions Russell expressed the view that his theory of descriptions was his most important contribution to philosophy. We can say that, from an extensional point of view, twelve years before Russell's first publication on the subject Frege had presented a superior treatment of it in his *Grundgesetze I* (1893). Still, Frege's treatment of descriptions is superior to Russell's only from an extensional point of view. It is only from the perspective of the intensional uses of the theory of descriptions that Russell's claims about the importance of his theory can be justified. This is the topic of chapter 4, below.

The Individuation of Intensions

Our discussions have repeatedly brought us to the problem of the individuation conditions for the intensions. Distrust of the use of intensions in philosophical analysis can, no doubt, be attributed largely to unclarity about this matter. Yet this is not an irremediable situation. It is not the case that it is somehow intrinsic to the nature of intensional concepts that they cannot be clearly individuated. In earlier passages in this chapter I have reported some of my own intuitions concerning identity and difference of properties and propositions. I would be surprised if these were not generally shared. The task is to reach a formulation of these and similar intuitions that is suitable for our purpose: an account of the logical form of statements of assertion and belief and of the propositional attitudes generally. In what follows I present some proposals that seem to me either to solve our problem or at least come close to doing so.

Classes and truth-values are extensions. Attributes (properties) and propositions are intensions. Relations may be understood either as relations in extension or as relations in intension. Individuals are extensions, and their corresponding individual concepts are intensions. Extensions generally are kinds of entities for which we can either state conditions for individuation that are clear and unproblematic or else the conditions for their individuation are sufficiently clear at the intuitive level for whatever purpose we have at hand. Classes are a kind of entity for which we can present a paradigmatic condition for individuation; two classes are identical if, and only if, they have the same members, so that, e.g., the class of human beings is the same as the class of rational animals. But what about the *attributes* of being a human being and being a rational animal? Presumably they are different though coextensive; for, if they are taken as the same, by the criterion of coextensiveness there is nothing to distinguish them from the corresponding classes. We have here a characteristic feature of the relationship between extensions and intensions. The same class is determined by different attributes. Two sentences may agree in extension (truth-value) and differ in intension (express different propositions). The same individual may be determined by many different individual concepts. *Intensions are more finely individuated than extensions.*

We have stated the identity-condition for classes as paradigmatic. Can we do the same for some kind of intensional entities? First, we may inquire why the condition given for classes is held to be adequate. The answer here is clear. If two classes satisfy the condition, have the same members, then any expression denoting one of these classes may replace any other expression denoting a class having the same members in any extensional context, *salva veritate*. A satisfactory condition individuating intensions of some kind must satisfy a similar requirement. Two names for the same attribute (or proposition, or individual concept) that satisfy the condition of individuation must be intersubstitutive, *salva veritate*, in intensional contexts of belief and assertion.

If we keep in mind the condition just stated for a satisfactory condition of individuation for intensions, we can see why intensional contexts are generally divided into two main categories. One category consists of the contexts of alethic modality (necessity, possibility, impossibility, contingency); the other consists of the propositional attitudes (in the first place, belief). For contexts of alethic modality, propositions are identified by the condition of logical equivalence, i.e., by the condition of having the same truth-value as a matter of logic alone. Thus, in a modal logic whose underlying extensional fragment is that of classical first-order quantification theory, unmodalized propositions are identified that satisfy the condition of logical equivalence within that first-order fragment. Sentences that express propositions that are equivalent (by classical first-order logic) are everywhere intersubstitutive in modal contexts. The condition may be extended to unmodalized attributes, and to relations generally, as follows: relations in intension are identical that provably have the same extension by classical first-order logic. For individual concepts again the analogous condition is correct: individual concepts are identical that provably are concepts of the same individual by first-order logic with identity.

For the general case, including that of propositions, propositional functions, and other intensions that are modalized—i.e., for the case of those intensions whose linguistic expression involves the use of modal operators—the situation is complicated by the existence of several alternative conceptions of the modalities to be considered—by many alternative formalizations of modal logic. Still, the general form of the required extension is this: Sentences that express propositions that are logically equivalent according to the formulation of the logic of modality under consideration are to be regarded as expressing the same proposition. The extension of this principle to other intensions—to propositional functions of arbitrary degree and to individual concepts—is then routine. Alternative conceptions of modality yield alternative individuation conditions and hence alternative conceptions of the intensions.

The difficult problem of individuation for intensions arises in connection with the propositional attitudes, not in connection with alethic modality. The first major step toward a resolution of this difficulty was taken by Rudolf Carnap in *Meaning and Necessity* with his introduction of the concept of *intensional isomorphism*. It is clear that the condition of logical equivalence, adequate for modal contexts, is too weak for belief contexts. Even persons of extraordinary logical powers may fail to recognize two logically equivalent propositions as logically equivalent and may hence believe one and not the other. If, on the other hand, we recognize that there is no limit to the level of logical incompetence, it becomes problematic whether any condition of individuation for intensions can be formulated that will not be too strong. It will be instructive to consider this matter in the context of specific proposals.

In the discussion of intensional isomorphism we shall be concerned both with the intensions of the designators that compose a sentence and with the manner in which the sentence is built up out of these designators. In Carnap's words, "If two sentences are built in the same way out of corresponding designators with the same intensions, then we shall say that they have the same intensional structure" (Carnap, [*MN*], p. 56). Here are some examples. Carnap considers the expressions '2 + 5' and 'II sum V'. These occur in a language *S,* in which '2', '5', 'II', 'V', are numerical expressions and '+', 'sum', are signs for the operation of addition. We suppose that, according to the semantical rules of *S,* '2' is L-equivalent to 'II', '5' to 'V', and '+' to 'sum'. Now, Carnap says, ". . . we shall say that the two expressions are *intensionally isomorphic* or that they have *the same intensional structure,* because they are not only L-equivalent as a whole, both being L-equivalent to '7', but consist of three parts in such a way that corresponding parts are L-equivalent to one another and hence have the same intension" (ibid.). In this example, the corresponding parts have corresponding positions from left to right in their respective expressions. What is desired, however, is a relation of correspondence that is syntactical and not merely spatial. Thus Carnap regards '5 > 3' and 'Gr (V,III)' as intensionally isomorphic because the predicators '>' and 'Gr' are L-equivalent and so are '5' and 'V', and '3' and 'III'. The predicators are corresponding parts because of their syntactical role, even though one occurs in the middle of the sentence containing it and the other at the beginning. '2 + 5 > 3' is intensionally isomorphic to 'Gr [sum (II,V),III]' because '2 + 5' is intensionally isomorphic to 'sum (II,V)', the predicators are L-equivalent, and so are the corresponding signs for the operation of addition, as well as '3' and 'III'. On the other hand, '7 > 3' is not intensionally isomorphic to 'Gr[sum(II,V),III]' even though 'Gr' is L-equivalent to '>', '3' to 'III', and 'sum (II, V)' to '7'. They are not intensionally isomorphic because 'sum(II,V)' is not intensionally isomorphic to '7', although they are L-equivalent and hence have the same intension. Isomorphism of two expressions requires the isomorphism of all corresponding subdesignators.

Carnap's actual definition of intensional isomorphism is stated with respect to designator matrices, containing free variables. Since the definition does not claim to be exact, it will not be presented here. Carnap says, "The present definition makes no claim to exactness; an exact definition would have to refer to one or two semantical systems whose rules are stated completely" (ibid., p. 58). Still it is clear what Carnap's concept is. The problem is to give it a precise formulation within the setting of a formalized language. First, however, we will continue to examine the concept at an informal level, to make sure that it does indeed serve as an adequate criterion for the individuation of intensions.

Carnap intends his concept to have application to well-formed formulas containing free variables. Two designator matrices (well-formed formulas containing free variables), A and B, are said to be L-equivalent if, and only if, the universal closure of $A \equiv B$ is L-true. Two designator matrices containing the same free variables are said to be intensionally isomorphic if one can be obtained from the other by a series of transformations that consist of (1) alphabetic change of bound variables, (2) substitution of one individual constant by an

L-equivalent one, (3) substitution of one predicator constant by an L-equivalent one.*

Intensional isomorphism is intended by Carnap to serve as a criterion of identity for the objects of belief, propositions. Alonzo Church has presented convincing reasons to suppose that, as such, it is too weak, but he has also recommended modifications of it that apparently do provide an adequate condition of individuation for propositions as objects of belief and other propositional attitudes (Church, [IIIB], pp. 65–73). Church's proposal is to change conditions (2) and (3) in the above characterization of Carnap's concept by *replacing the requirement of L-equivalence by that of synonymy*. The resulting concept is Church's concept of *synonymous isomorphism*. To motivate the change, Church gives the following example. In a language like Carnap's S_1, in which the individuals are the positive integers, let P and Q be predicator constants such that Pn expresses that $n < 3$, and Qn expresses that there exist x, y, and z such that $x^n + y^n = z^n$. P and Q are introduced into the language as primitive constants, perhaps with axioms such as may be suggested by their meanings. For the purpose of the example, Church supposes that indeed Fermat did have a proof for his famous Last Theorem, so that P and Q are L-equivalent. We may, for the sake of the example, assume that the axioms allow us to prove that $(n)(Pn \equiv Qn)$. Yet it is clear that one might believe that $(\exists n)(Qn .\sim Pn)$ and not believe $(\exists n)(Pn .\sim Pn)$, since, as Church remarks, ". . . the proof of Fermat's Last Theorem, though it is possible, is certainly difficult to find (as the history of the matter shows)" (ibid., p. 66). The two formulas are intensionally isomorphic but not synonymously isomorphic, so Church's modification is clearly an improvement. Analogous considerations concerning other kinds of designators lead to additions to (1) and the modified conditions (2), and (3), above, so that the following kinds of replacements shall also be allowed: "(4) *replacement of an abstraction expression by a synonymous predicator constant;* (5) *replace-*

---

* This simplified form of the definition of 'intensionally isomorphic' follows Church rather than Carnap. For present purposes we confine our attention to a single language, Carnap's S_1 with added constants, and to designator matrices within S_1 containing the same free variables (Church, [IIIB], pp. 65–66). It is because of these restrictions that the definition can be given in this simplified form (ibid., p. 71, n. 5).

ment of a predicator constant by a synonymous abstraction expression;
(6) *replacement of an individual description by a synonymous individual constant;* (7) *replacement of an individual constant by a synonymous individual description"* (Church, ibid., p. 67).

Thus Church proposes synonymous isomorphism as a criterion of identity of beliefs. To make use of this criterion, it will be necessary to provide rules that directly or indirectly determine which expressions of the language are to be taken as synonymous. The rules are to be constructed so as to satisfy such requirements as that of noncircularity and consistency. In a formalized language containing individual and predicate constants some synonymies may be directly stipulated outright, e.g., 'succulent' and 'juicy', 'erotic' and 'sexy', 'Los Angeles' and 'L.A.'. Using the list of stipulated synonymies, it can then be determined which complex expressions are synonymously isomorphic, i.e., are transformable into each other by replacement of parts by synonymous parts. An objection is sometimes made to the use of directly stipulated synonymies (Carnap calls them "meaning postulates") on the ground that such lists are just lists headed by the words 'synonymies' or 'meaning postulates'. It is then said that these terms are unclear and in need of analysis and that the giving of such lists does not make them any clearer and is, in any case, no substitute for philosophical analysis of them. Of course, the list is headed not by the word 'synonymies' but by 'synonymies (in L)', where L is the formalized language being constructed. The situation is exactly the same with 'definitions' and 'axioms'. They too are given by lists headed by these terms as applied to a specified language. Surely there can be no methodological objection to definition by enumeration. Of course, the formal languages we wish to consider are constructed as idealized models of some parts of natural language. That is the interest they have for us. So presumably the objection is that the word 'synonymy' is so unclear as to be completely devoid of any meaning at all as a term of natural language. That seems to me a philosopher's extreme position and hardly an established truth. At any rate, the position of this book is that the notion of synonymy is neither unintelligible nor useless and that the stipulation of pairs of expressions as synonyms is well-enough understood as a formal counterpart to our informal concept.

A persistent charge against the legitimacy of intensions has been that they are "creatures of darkness" because of an absence of clarity concerning their identity-conditions. It would seem, however, that the actual situation is one in which we are presented with a number of alternative identity-conditions and that the problem is to determine which is the most suitable. It may then appear that our inability to choose among logical equivalence, intensional isomorphism, synonymous isomorphism, and perhaps others reflects a lack of clarity about the nature of the entities with which we purport to be dealing. I would suggest an alternative way of looking at this situation. My suggestion is that we are dealing simply with alternative conceptions of the intensions corresponding to the alternative conditions of individuation. Suppose it is asked how many words ("word-types") Milton used in *Paradise Lost*. If one proceeds to determine the answer to this question by counting, one will use a different criterion of individuation for word-types than one would use in determining the number of different "words" (tokens) that work contains for the purpose of calculating the amount of ink needed to reprint it. Does this reflect an unclarity about the nature of the entity that concerns us? Not at all, for we are talking about different kinds of entity, corresponding to the different criteria of individuation—one criterion for word-types, the other for word-tokens. Similarly, I suggest that there are different conceptions of propositions corresponding to the alternative conditions of individuation. The propositions of alethic modal logic (individuated by logical equivalence) are different entities from the propositions individuated by the condition of synonymous isomorphism. Both are equally legitimate. It is not a matter of competing conditions of individuation for one kind of entity; it is a matter of different kinds of entities, individuated by different conditions.

Summary and Conclusion for Chapters 1 and 2

By a "form of Frege's puzzle" is meant an identity-statement that is both true and informative. Each type of designator that may appropriately flank the identity-sign to form identity-statements yields a class of candidates for a form of Frege's puzzle. In *Principia*-like notation, the following forms have been considered:

(1) $S = (\imath x)(Wx)$
(2) $p = q$
(3) $\hat{x}(\phi x) = \hat{x}(\psi x)$
(4) $\phi\hat{x} = \psi\hat{x}$
(5) $a = b$
(6) $N_1 = N_2$

Frege's solution to his puzzle is this: If our identity-statement is true, the designators flanking the sign of identity have the same reference. If it is also informative, these designators are different in sense. This combination of identity of reference and difference of sense explains the possibility of informative statements of identity.

Russell's theory rejects the notion of sense. He deals with the problem of true and informative identity-statements while first granting that there cannot be any. Frege's puzzle, for Russell, is based on a logical mirage. Statements of the kind (5), above, contain two logically proper names. If such statements are true, they are not informative. A proper name "means" what it denotes. Hence, if (5) is true, both 'a' and 'b' denote the same thing and '$a = b$' denotes the same proposition as '$a = a$'. Statements of the kind (1) may be both true and informative, but they are not identities, because of the contained description. The same can be said of (3), since class abstracts are incomplete symbols, which do not appear in the underlying logical form of the statement. This leaves statements of the kind (2), (4), and (6).

Russell's solution to Frege's puzzle, in the forms already considered, involves two claims. First, every informative identity contains an incomplete symbol, contextually defined. Second, when the incomplete symbol is eliminated in accordance with its contextual definition, it is shown that the purported informative identity is not logically an identity.

With regard to form (2) of Frege's puzzle, we have argued that the substituends for 'p' and 'q' are *not* incomplete symbols, for they denote propositions, and propositions must be admitted as part of the ultimate logical furniture of the *Principia* universe. The same holds for statements of the form (4); propositional functions, too, belong to the ultimate logical furniture of the world.

Do statements of the form (2) and (4) then yield forms of Frege's puzzle that cannot be eliminated? Now there emerges an interesting relation between Frege's solution to his puzzle and the Russellian solution such that, if the one solution is acceptable, so must the other be. For Frege, informative identities involve identity of reference and difference of sense. Hence, for case (2), they involve identity of truth-value denoted and difference of thoughts (propositions) expressed. We can associate the different propositions expressed on the Fregean view with the different propositions denoted on the Russellian view. Of course, from the inside, so to speak, Fregean propositions (thoughts) look different from Russellian propositions. The constituents of a Fregean proposition belong to "the realm of sense," while the constituents of a Russellian proposition are the objects, propositional functions, and propositions denoted by the logically relevant units composing the sentence that denotes the proposition. The constituents of a Russellian proposition belong to "the realm of reference." Nevertheless, we can associate, one to one, Fregean thoughts with Russellian propositions. The two thoughts expressed, on Frege's view, in a case (2) form of Frege's puzzle are associated with the two propositions denoted on Russell's analysis of this purported form of Frege's puzzle. Hence, an identity of form (2) is, for Russell, false, if, for Frege, it is informative, and so it is not a form of Frege's puzzle for Russell after all. Thus, if the one solution works, so does the other.

Are the two solutions equally adequate? Frege acknowledges as truths, statements that Russell regards as false. Take again our example of the axiom of choice and the well-ordering principle. The identity-statement formed from two sentences expressing these propositions is true for Frege and false for Russell. Nevertheless, the two views agree on all the facts, so to speak; they differ only about how to formulate them. For truth, Frege requires only identity of truth-value, and Russell expresses this as the truth of a material biconditional. Thus Russell can acknowledge the same body of truths of the form $p = q$ as Frege does, only he formulates them as being of the form $p \equiv q$.

A similar account can be given of cases of the kind (4). These cannot arise for Frege, of course, since identity is not for him a relation that holds between concepts. What, for Russell, is a statement of identity of propositional functions (case 4) is expressed in Frege's Begriffsschrift as a statement of coextension of concepts. *Identity* of concepts (and of functions generally) is not, for Frege, expressible at all. Hence there is not, for him, any problem about cases of the puzzle of type (4). In the body of this chapter I dealt with the question whether there are, for Russell, cases of Frege's puzzle of this kind that cannot be eliminated, and I concluded that we would be unlikely to find any. Any identity of the form $\phi\hat{x} = \psi\hat{x}$ that, intuitively, is informative would, for that very reason, count as not true. Any acceptable criterion for identity of properties (attributes, propositional functions in intension) should be in accord with these intuitions.

Case (6) above, $N_1 = N_2$, is an identity-statement in which the letters 'N_1' and 'N_2' are meant to represent proper names ordinarily so-called—names such as 'Hesperus' and 'Phosphorus', 'Cicero' and 'Tully'; i.e., not logically proper names. Take, then, as our sample case 'Hesperus = Phosphorus'. For Russell, these names are disguised descriptions, so our identity is of the form $(\imath x)(\phi x) = (\imath x)(\psi x)$; thus this case, on his view, reduces to a special case of type (1). For Frege, the different senses of these names become their denotations in oblique contexts such as 'George IV wished to know whether Hesperus = Phosphorus.' The senses of these names are atomic—lacking in relevant semantic structure, just as the names themselves lack relevant syntactic structure. Definite descriptions expressing the same atomic senses are 'the hesperizer' $[(\imath x)(x = $ Hesperus$)]$; 'the phosphorizer' $[(\imath x)(x = $ Phosphorus$)]$. In thus interpreting these descriptions, the sign of identity is to be thought of not as an independent binary-relation sign but as an indissoluble part of the predicate, 'is-Hesperus', 'is-Phosphorus'. These propositional functions, $\hat{x}$ hesperizes, $\hat{x}$ phosphorizes, are satisfied by one thing, Hesperus (= Phosphorus). In Russell's view these propositional functions are the objects denoted in sentences containing the names 'Hesperus' and 'Phosphorus'. This is revealed once these names are eliminated in accordance with the theory of descriptions.

Russell's theory of oblique contexts, at this point, looks remarkably like Frege's theory. It appears that we can form something like a mapping of Fregean senses onto Russellian intensions in such a way as to produce a transformation of the Fregean solution for an intensional paradox into a Russellian solution. Ordinary names—'Homer', 'Cicero', 'Tully'—correspond to Russellian descriptions using the device invented by Quine: 'socratizes'. What is required is a propositional function that is satisfied by at most one object; for the sense of a name, for Frege, is a concept of at most one object. (In the ideal language we could say, "of exactly one object." At this point we want to allow for names that lack a denotation, hence have vacuous senses.) So the way to effect the transformation is this. First determine the Fregean sense of the name. This (effectively) yields the Russellian propositional function. Just as this sense becomes the reference in a Fregean analysis of oblique contexts, so the Russellian corresponding propositional function becomes the denotation of the name or description in the same intensional context. (I owe this idea of mapping Fregean solutions of intensional paradoxes onto Russellian ones and conversely to Church's unpublished address to the American Philosophical Association in San Diego in 1979.)

If, with Frege, logic is made completely extensional, intensional contexts must be set aside for special treatment. This course makes the subsequent adoption of the sense/reference distinction almost inevitable. If, with Russell, the sense/reference distinction is rejected, then intensional contexts can't be set aside for special treatment. The course of adapting an intensional logic from the beginning is again almost inevitable. Now one *can* both insist on a policy of extensionality in logic and reject the sense/reference distinction. But only, it would seem, by turning one's back on the phenomenon of intensionality altogether. One might deny that intensional contexts have intelligible logical structure at all and top this off by giving them a bad name: "opaque." This is the course that Quine, in some of his writings, seems to advocate.

3

Indirect Sense and Reference

I

According to Frege, names in indirect (oblique) contexts have indirect senses and indirect references rather than their customary or vulgar ones. In the context of direct quotation, too, words do not have their customary senses and references. Nor do they here have their indirect senses and references either. Rather, these words refer to themselves. In the terminology of the Scholastic logicians, in direct quotation words have *suppositio materialis;* they refer to themselves. Words in vulgar occurrences have *suppositio formalis;* they have their customary references. Frege and the medieval logicians agree in regarding quotation as a *construction* in which quoted material occurs in a semantically relevant way. Their view is opposed to Quine's "orthographic-accident" interpretation. According to this, within quotation words occur as mere accidents of spelling, no more logically germane than the occurrence of 'cat' within 'cattle' (Quine, [TGMI], p. 161). The only semantically relevant unit, on this view, is the whole quotation, including the outermost pair of quotation marks. Quotation, thus, is not a grammatical construction but a logically homogeneous whole without relevant parts. Names within quotation, on this view, are rendered semantically inert—they do not denote at all—and quotation is therefore the "referentially opaque" context *par excellence*.

When Quine comes to deal with belief-contexts and indirect quotation, he tends to assimilate them to direct quotation, at least on this score: these contexts, too, are referentially opaque, and names within them are semantically and logically impotent. On this view, belief-contexts and indirect-discourse contexts, like direct-discourse contexts, lack relevant logical and semantic structure. When Frege, by contrast, turns to indirect-discourse contexts, belief-contexts, and propositional-attitude contexts generally, he adheres to the already exhibited policy of positing relevant semantic structure as generously as possible. He finds here not opacity and impotence but, rather, obliquity and referential shift. In an indirect context of belief, or *oratio obliqua,* the indirect reference of a name becomes its customary sense. The sense of a name in an indirect context, accordingly, is its indirect sense. The indirect reference of a name is its customary sense; but sense determines reference, and therefore the indirect sense of a name must differ from its customary sense. It is a new entity. We have here an application of Frege's context principle: only in the context of a sentence does a name have a reference. We cannot speak of *the* reference of a name, for that changes with the context, and the same is true of sense. The same name has different senses in a vulgar context, in a quotation context, and in *oratio obliqua.* The sense of the name in quotation is neither its customary sense nor its indirect sense (Frege does not give it a name).

Frege's view that words in indirect discourse undergo reference shift has an immediate intuitive and satisfying explanatory power. If I say, 'The earth moves', I am talking about the earth. The reference of my words is what I am talking about. But if I say, 'Galileo said that the earth moves', I am talking about what Galileo said and not about the earth. Here my aim is to convey to you the sense of Galileo's words. Hence the reference of my words—what I am talking about— is the sense of his words. My indirect-discourse report of what Galileo said is true just in case the sense that is the reference of my words, in my indirect discourse, is the same as the sense of the words he used directly to talk about the earth. If, instead of indirect discourse, I choose direct quotation to report (falsely) that Galileo said, 'The earth moves', it is perhaps even more obvious that my words, 'the earth', do not have their customary reference; they refer to themselves instead.

If we now ask why names that, in vulgar contexts, have the same reference fail of substitutivity, *salva veritate,* in indirect contexts, the immediate intuitive appeal of the above observations is carried over to Frege's explanation. We are not, according to him, faced with violations of Leibniz's Law in these cases but merely with ambiguity. Names in indirect contexts have a different reference (and consequently a different sense) from what they have in direct contexts. Hence failure of substitutivity on the basis of identity of customary reference is only to be expected. A wrong view of Frege's explanation reverses the order here. According to this, Frege first designed an account of sense and reference to fit the vulgar cases, and this account was shipwrecked on the banks of indirect discourse. Then Frege complicated his simple and plausible initial theory with the epicycles of reference shift and the new concepts of indirect sense and reference in order to rescue from paradox the work he had already done. What is wrong with this view is that it makes the complexities in Frege's account of the indirect cases appear *ad hoc*. It fails to appreciate how highly satisfying Frege's explanation of these cases really is.

Moreover, there seems to be an equally intuitive extension of Frege's account to cases of embeddings of names in multiply indirect contexts. If I say, 'Galileo said that the earth moves', the reference of my words 'the earth' is not to themselves, for Galileo spoke no English; the reference of my words is to the vulgar sense of the words 'the earth', for I intend to convey the sense of Galileo's Italian words. If I say, rather, 'Davidson said that Galileo said that the earth moves', there seems *prima facie* to be another shift of reference; for now I aim to convey the sense of Davidson's words, not Galileo's. Davidson spoke the truth if, and only if, the reference of his words, in the singly indirect context in which he reports what Galileo said, is the customary sense of Galileo's words. Suppose that Davidson did not speak the truth. Still, I speak the truth when I say, 'Davidson said that Galileo said that the earth moves'. My words refer to the sense of Davidson's words, not the sense of Galileo's. What we have here, then, is not proof that the words 'the earth', spoken by Davidson, have a different reference (and hence a different sense) from those words spoken by me but rather a very persuasive analogy between singly indirect-discourse cases and doubly indirect cases. Just as Davidson's words have a different reference (and hence a different sense) from Galileo's when he reports what Galileo said, so my words have a different reference (and a different sense) from Davidson's when I, in turn, report what he said. Further, just as the reference of Davidson's words is their customary sense and the sense of his words is their (singly) indirect sense, so the reference of my words is naturally taken to be this same singly indirect sense, and the sense of my words is accordingly their (doubly) indirect sense. A similar shift of reference (and hence of sense) should then be repeated with each new iteration.

The theory as Frege presented it in "On Sense and Reference" does not endorse such an extension for cases of multiply indirect contexts, for Frege here attributes to words just two senses, customary and indirect. But in a letter to Russell, written in 1902, he does argue for a hierarchy of indirect references in the account of contexts involving iterated operators of indirect discourse in natural language. In this connection, he contrasts the first-degree indirect reference with the second-degree indirect reference of a name. Since the argument for the distinction can be generalized for any finite number of indirect-discourse embeddings, it is reasonable to conclude that Frege, at least implicitly, commits himself in this letter to the infinite hierarchy of indirect senses and references associated with each name.

> Let, e.g., '*M*' and '*N*' (in direct speech) be names of the same class, so that $M = N$ is the true. . . . Since '*M*' has different meanings [*Bedeutungen*] in its two occurrences in the proposition 'the thought that *all thoughts belonging to the class M are true* does not belong to the class *M*', there must also be a difference in the meanings [*Bedeutungen*] of '*M*' in the expression 'the thought that *the thought that ALL THOUGHTS BELONGING TO THE CLASS M ARE TRUE does not belong to the class M*'. It can be said that in the twice-underlined part [printed here in italic capitals] it has an indirect meaning [*Bedeutung*] of the second degree, whereas in the once-underlined part [printed here in lowercase italic letters] it has an indirect meaning [*Bedeutung*] of the first degree. [Frege, [*PMC*], pp. 153–54]

Frege, in this passage, mentions only indirect references of different degrees, but it must be assumed that he intends the argument to justify indirect senses of different degrees as well. Frege here presents a persuasive analogy rather than a conclusive argument.

These shifts can be represented by Parsons-like diagrams that illustrate the beginning stages of an infinite hierarchy of senses and references. Let us abbreviate 'the customary sense of the word W' by '$s_1[W]$' and 'the customary reference of W' by '$r_1[W]$'. Let 'R' abbreviate the sentence 'the earth moves'. The semantics of the sentence R, in isolation, is represented in the following diagram:

$$s_1[R]$$

$$R$$

$$r_1[R]$$

The upward arrow represents the relation of 'expressing' and the sentence R expresses the thought that R ($= s_1[R]$). The lower arrow represents the denotation-relation; the sentence R denotes the truth-value thereof that R ($= r_1[R]$).

The semantics of 'Galileo said that the earth moves' is given by the diagram on the left on page 49. Here $s_2[R]$ = the indirect sense of 'R' that 'R' expresses in the singly indirect context 'Galileo said that R', and 'S' abbreviates 'Galileo said that'. The indirect reference of 'R' is its customary sense ($s_1[R]$). The reference of the whole sentence is obtained by applying the customary reference of 'S' to the singly indirect reference of 'R'. This application of function to argument is indicated by the parenthesis. And the value of this function for that argument is the truth-value indicated by the curly brackets: $\underset{Z}{\underbrace{X(Y)}}$ indicates that $Z = X(Y)$.

The doubly indirect context is then represented on the right on page 49.

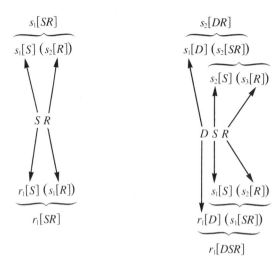

This diagram illustrates the iterated application of Frege's dual compositional principles, according to which the sense (reference) of a complex linguistic whole is determined by a function-argument combination of the senses (references) of its components. Frege associates with every complex linguistic expression three levels of the distinction between completeness and incompleteness. There is the distinction at the level of the expressions themselves, at the level of reference, and, finally, at the level of sense. Our diagram assumes that the sense of a (declarative) sentence, a complete sense, is composed of one or more complete senses associated with the complete names contained in the sentence and one or more incomplete senses associated with the incomplete names that can be extracted from the sentence. At the level of reference, the distinction between completeness and incompleteness coincides with the distinction between object and function. This is certainly not the case at the level of the expressions themselves. But what about the distinction between completeness and incompleteness at the level of sense? Is an incomplete sense a function? Frege never says that it is. Nevertheless, this is assumed here, and the assumption is to be used in interpreting these diagrams. Further, this assumption is used in the contemporary formulations of the logic of sense and denotation by Church and Anderson.

In addition to the dual compositional principles, the construction of our diagrams illustrates the working of the Fregean principles (*a*) that in direct contexts words have their direct senses and references, (*b*) that in indirect contexts of degree *n* they have their indirect senses and references of degree *n;* and, finally, (*c*) that the indirect reference of degree *n* is the same as the indirect sense of degree $n - 1$, while the indirect sense of degree *n* is a new entity. (My discussion of the diagrams adheres closely to Terence Parsons' paper [FHIS].)

II

I have emphasized the intuitions behind Frege's treatment of oblique contexts, which make the account very persuasive. Frege did not work out the details of his theory to the point of presenting it in logistic form, and subsequent attempts to do so have met with considerable difficulty. At the same time, others have not agreed that the underlying intuitions that guide Frege are correct, and they present arguments against his view. Here I would like to consider one alternative theory of oblique contexts—that of Dummett.

In a passage in *Meaning and Necessity* in which Carnap compares his own theory with Frege's, he remarks that one difference "is brought about by Frege's differentiation between the ordinary and oblique sense of a name" (Carnap, [*MN*], p. 129). He then goes on to say, "It is not easy to say what his reasons were for regarding them as different. . . . It does not appear, at least not to me, that it would be unnatural or implausible to ascribe its ordinary sense to a name in an oblique context," and he concludes: "Incidentally, it seems that Frege nowhere explains in more customary terms what this third entity is."

Dummett agrees with Carnap in objecting to the introduction of a hierarchy of indirect senses of expressions. "What then," he asks, "is the indirect sense of an expression? Frege has told us what its indirect referent is, namely its ordinary sense; but that is not enough to determine what its indirect sense is to be. It is clear that there is no way available to state what the *sense* of an expression when it occurs in opaque contexts is to be taken to be" (Dummett, [*Frege*], p. 267). This seems to me a mistaken criticism. Dummett objects that there is no way to *state* what the sense of an expression in indirect discourse is to be taken to be. This is in a way correct, but the same "criticism" can be directed against the sense of an expression in a vulgar context. What is it to be taken to be? One can say that it is to be taken to be a criterion of identification of the customary reference of a name. And the indirect sense is likewise a criterion of identification of a customary sense.

Dummett observes (ibid.) that "there is no backward road" from reference to sense. That is because sense determines reference and not conversely. But there is a mistake in Dummett's implied requirement that we should be able to "state" what the sense of any expression is, and this applies as well to customary as to indirect sense. Sense is what our words express. (A Stoic *dictum:* Sense is what the Greeks grasp and the barbarians don't when Greek words are spoken.) There is no concept of sense except as that which words can or do express. Thus the only manner in which a sense can be presented, so to speak, is by the use of words that express this sense. There is no alternative nonlinguistic route to it. Thus some critics have objected that ordinary proper names do not have senses, for they ask "What is the sense, e.g., of 'Adam' supposed to be?" And indeed, the question is disconcerting, for there seems to be no way to say what the sense is. But, neither can we say what the sense of 'the king of France' is, and descriptive phrases are admitted to be paradigms of expressions having sense. Of course the request might be for a translation, say into Italian. 'The king of France' has the same sense as 'Il re di Francia'. But 'Adam' can as well be translated: 'Adamo'. In any case, I see no merit in Dummett's invidious comparison between customary and indirect senses on this score.

Dummett, however, believes that a simple emendation of Frege's theory will free it of the blemish of indirect sense. He says, "The whole difficulty arises from the principle that the reference of an expression must be determined from the sense alone" (ibid.). This is of course correct. Sense determines reference. Hence if reference shifts from vulgar to indirect contexts, sense must as well. What Dummett proposes is to make reference determined by sense plus context so that a name will have a single sense that determines it to have different references in direct and indirect contexts. According to

Frege's "context principle," a word has a reference only in the context of a sentence. Dummett says, "It is fully harmonious with this view to hold that, while a word or expression *by itself* has a sense, it does not by itself have a reference at all: only a particular occurrence of a word or expression in a sentence has a reference, and this reference is determined jointly by the sense of the word and the kind of context in which it occurs" (ibid., p. 268).

With this emendation the indirect sense drops out of consideration. For Dummett there is just the sense of a word, which determines it to have (*a*) in transparent contexts a reference distinct from its sense and (*b*) in indirect contexts a referent that coincides with its sense. "There is therefore no reason to think that an expression occurring in double *oratio obliqua* has a sense or a reference different from that which it has in single *oratio obliqua:* its referent in double *oratio obliqua* will be the sense which it has in single *oratio obliqua,* which is the same as the sense it has in ordinary contexts, which is the same as its referent in single *oratio obliqua*" (ibid., pp. 268–69). For this emendation to work, what is required is that substitutivity, *salva veritate,* for names in doubly indirect contexts should occur under exactly the same condition under which it occurs for names in singly indirect contexts, viz., when the terms have the same customary sense. Clearly this condition is satisfied, so Dummett concludes: "The view that doubly indirect sense and reference must be distinguished from simply indirect sense and reference was a mechanical deduction from a slightly faulty theory" (ibid., p. 269).

My reaction to Dummett's emendation of Frege is that it is unnecessary. The indirect sense of a term is no more mysterious an entity than the direct sense. Further, whatever reason there is for maintaining a reference shift from transparent to singly indirect contexts applies again to the shift from singly indirect to doubly indirect contexts, and so on up. Finally, it seems to me that Dummett's emendation is merely verbal. What he calls "the sense" of a name is just the infinite hierarchy of Frege's indirect senses collected together. The sense, in Dummett's "sense," is just the collection of all the indirect senses that Frege requires. If it is not that, it will not serve the purposes of the infinite hierarchy. Of course, the converse is also true. Frege's infinite hierarchy of indirect senses can be identified with Dummett's single sense simply by collecting the individual indirect senses of a name into *one* new object, *the* sense.

I believe, in any case, that the issue between Dummett's truncated hierarchy and Frege's suggested infinite hierarchy cannot be settled or even advanced by appeal to intuitions about examples from every-day language. Consider the sentences 'The earth rotates' and 'The earth turns', and let us assume that they have the same (customary) sense and reference. Then, in the indirect context 'Galileo said that the earth rotates', we should, according to Dummett's theory, be able to replace 'rotates' by 'turns', while preserving sense, and obtain 'Galileo said that the earth turns'. Surely there is no conflict here with linguistic intuition. But there is a just as adequate Fregean expla-nation of the same phenomenon. This explanation invokes the con-sideration that 'rotates' and 'turns' share not only their customary sense but their (first-degree) indirect sense as well. It is this latter sense that they have in the indirect contexts. Dummett observes that names agreeing in customary sense are intersubstitutive, *salva veri-tate*, in *any* indirect context, no matter how many iterations of indirect-discourse operators the sentence contains. For example, 'Davidson said that Galileo said that the earth rotates' has the same sense as 'Davidson said that Galileo said that the earth turns'. Dum-mett's explanation would be that the terms 'rotates' and 'turns' have the same sense—their customary sense—also in this doubly indirect context. It is for this reason that he sees no need to invoke an indirect sense. But again, there is an entirely adequate Fregean account of this case as well. It is that just as 'rotates' and 'turns' share their custom-ary and (first-degree) indirect sense, so do they share their second-degree indirect sense, and so on up, *ad infinitum*. This Fregean theory accords as well as Dummett's with intuition. Linguistic intuition cannot decide the issue. I now turn to a consideration of ontological economy.

III

A principal motive behind proposals, like Dummett's, to truncate the infinite hierarchy of indirect senses in Frege's semantics, and even to eliminate from it altogether the notion of indirect sense, is one of economy. A singly indirect sense is a concept of a customary sense, and a doubly indirect sense is a concept of a singly indirect sense, and so on *ad infinitum,* with concepts of concepts of concepts . . . . Even in such abstract matters as the present one, however, there is such a thing as false economy; for some form of the infinite hierarchy of senses and senses of senses is necessary if we are to avoid reintroducing cases of Frege's puzzle like those that motivated him to introduce the sense/reference distinction in the first place. To see this, consider an instance of the puzzle '*A* = *B*' where '*A*' and '*B*' denote objects of lowest logical type. This, we will suppose, is informative, because, although '*A*' and '*B*' agree in reference, they differ in sense. Now nothing prevents our language from containing another name (with another sense) for the sense of *A;* say '*C*'. And now we can raise Frege's question again: How can '*C* = the sense of '*A*' ' differ in cognitive value, if true, from '*C* = *C*'? The Fregean answer is that '*C*' and 'the sense of '*A*' ' agree in reference but differ in sense. The reference of '*C*' is the sense of '*A*', and the sense of '*C*' is a concept of the sense of '*A*'; thus it is a sense of the sense of '*A*'. In this way we generate our hierarchy of senses, senses of senses, senses of senses of senses, *ad infinitum.*

In this example, '*C*' is meant to stand for an arbitrary singular term whose reference is a sense, not necessarily an atomic singular term— i.e., a proper name. To take a particular case from natural language, consider this: The sense of 'red' in English = the sense of 'rouge' in French. This is a true identity and different in cognitive value from: The sense of 'red' in English = the sense of 'red' in English. The two terms, 'the sense of 'red' in English' and 'the sense of 'rouge' in French', both denote a sense (the same sense) and express a sense (different senses). The sense they denote is a concept of a sense, thus a sense of a sense. My contention is that it is part of the spirit of natural language to allow for the construction of such names at any level in the sense hierarchy, so that to truncate the hierarchy at any level is to leave open the possibility of introducing forms of Frege's puzzle about identity at that level, while depriving ourselves of Frege's solution to his puzzle. Moreover, if we use the accepted conventions governing the device of quotation, we can actually indicate a procedure that locates such expressions in a completely nonarbitrary way. In fact, it shows that these names can be constructed in English. They do not need to be introduced by special stipulation. Consider the statement,

(1) The sense of 'red', in English = the sense of 'rosso', in Italian.

Both terms denote the same sense, and each expresses a different concept of it; hence they express different concepts of the same concept. Now consider

(2) The sense of 'the sense of 'red', in English', in English = the sense of 'il senso de 'red', in Inglese', in Italian.

The term on the left side of (2) denotes the sense of the term on the left side of (1). The sense of the term on the left side of (1) is a concept of a concept. Hence the term on the left side of (2) denotes a concept of a concept and expresses a concept of a concept of a concept. The term on the right side of (2) denotes the same concept of a concept as the term on its left side, since (2) is true, but it expresses a different concept of it. Hence (2) has cognitive value and conveys genuine information. Now the same procedure that produces (2) out of (1) can be iterated *ad infinitum*, and it shows the need for the infinite sense hierarchy if we are to avoid unsolvable cases of Frege's puzzle.

The argument establishes the need for the infinite sense hierarchy. The need for this hierarchy remains even if we follow Dummett in truncating the infinite hierarchy of indirect senses by identifying the indirect and customary senses of names. Again, accepting the hierarchy of indirect sense does not expand our ontology, for these indirect senses can all be located in our present hierarchy of senses, senses of senses, etc. Now there is no reason for identifying the singly indirect sense of 'A', in our example above, with the customary sense of 'C', even though both of these senses are concepts of the customary sense of 'A'. Still, there are not two infinite hierarchies of senses to be considered but only one, and the attempt to remove it by identifying indirect and customary sense, as proposed by Dummett, is really a false economy.

IV

The Method of Indirect Discourse and the
Method of Direct Discourse

There is another approach, however—one that does eliminate indirect senses from the Fregean treatment of intensional contexts but does so without recourse to dismantling the infinite sense hierarchy. It has long been advocated by Church, and, in fact, it was Frege's idea in the first place. Frege introduces the concept of indirect sense in the context of a discussion of examples of indirect discourse taken from everyday, colloquial language. It is clear, however, that, had he gone on to incorporate the idiom of indirect discourse into a formal language, he would have dispensed with indirect sense in order to avoid ambiguity. In his letter to Russell dated December 28, 1902, already cited, Frege says, in this connection, "Eigentlich müsste man ja, um Zweideutigkeit zu vermeiden, in ungerader Rede besondere Zeichen haben, deren Zusammenhang aber mit den entsprechenden in gerader Rede leicht erkennbar wäre" [Really, in order to avoid ambiguity, one must, in indirect discourse, use special signs, whose association with those corresponding to them in direct discourse, however, would be easily recognizable] (Frege, [WB], p. 236). And Church proposes that "In a formalized logical system, a name would be represented by a distinct symbol in its ordinary and its oblique use" (Church, [Review Q], p. 46).

There are, then, in Frege's writings, indications, certainly not much elaborated—one might speak, rather, of hints—of two contrasting approaches to the analysis of oblique contexts. The *method of indirect discourse* is that suggested in his essay "On Sense and Reference," which, suitably generalized, leads to the infinite sequence of indirect senses attached to each name. The *method of direct discourse* is that suggested in the letter to Russell, which results from adopting, rather, an infinite sequence of new (but related) names associated with each name; the point was to eliminate the ambiguity connected with the first method. (The terms "the method of indirect discourse" and "the method of direct discourse" come from David Kaplan's dissertation *Foundations of Intensional Logic* [FIL]. The first chapter of Kaplan's work contains a valuable discussion of this distinction that has influenced the presentation given here.)

In the *method of indirect discourse,* which is suggested in Frege's informal discussions, each name has an infinite sequence of indirect senses and references associated with it. In the *direct-discourse method* it has a single sense and reference. This is achieved by the simple device of using a new name for each embedding within the scope of an indirect-discourse operator, e.g., *necessity.* Here is an example, from Church, comparing the workings of the two methods in connection with the use of a modal operator '$\diamond$' for *logical possibility.* In the method of indirect discourse the modal operator is prefixed to a *sentence,* so that, for example, if '$bi = h$' is a sentence that may be used to assert that the class of featherless bipeds is the same as the class of men, then '$\diamond bi = h$' is also a sentence that may be used to assert the possibility that the class of featherless bipeds is the same as the class of men. In the second method, modal operators are attached to *names* of propositions (senses), and the result of prefixing a modal operator to a sentence is not well formed. Instead of allowing the indirect use of expressions that occurs in '$\diamond bi = h$', we follow Frege's suggestion and introduce three new names, say, 'β', 'ι', and 'η' to denote the senses expressed by the names 'b', 'i', and 'h', respectively. Thus 'β', 'ι', and 'η' are names of concepts of the class of bipeds, featherless things, and men, respectively. We introduce two more signs, say 'ρ' and 'σ', to denote the sense of the sign of intersection (or logical product) of classes and the sense of the sign of identity ('$=$'), respectively. Consequently, '$\beta\rho\iota\sigma\eta$' is the name of the proposition (thought) expressed by the sentence '$bi = h$', and '$\diamond\beta\rho\iota\sigma\eta$' again is a sentence that may be used to assert the possibility that the class of featherless bipeds is the same as the class of men. (This example is taken from Alonzo Church, ["Postscript 1968"].) Note, then, that in this second method the whole hierarchy of indirect senses has simply disappeared.

From the premisses

(1) $bi = h$,

and

(2) $\sim\diamond\sim h = h$,

which we may suppose to be true, one may be puzzled as to why

(3) $\sim\diamond\sim bi = h,$

which is presumably false, does not follow by substitutivity of identity. One appreciates the extent to which the puzzle here is due to the ambiguous notation used in the method of indirect discourse as soon as our three sentences are replaced by the superior unambiguous notation of the direct-discourse method. Thus (letting $\square$ be the necessity operator of modal logic) there is no temptation whatever to suppose that, from

(1) $bi = h,$

and

(2′) $\square\eta\sigma\eta,$

there follows, by substitutivity of identity,

(3′) $\square\beta\rho\iota\sigma\eta.$

On the other hand, in spite of (1),

(4) $\beta\rho\iota = \eta$

expresses a false proposition.

V

(Declarative) Sentences Denote Truth-Values

For Frege, the reference of a (declarative) sentence is its truth-value. Accordingly, all true sentences denote the same thing, "the True," and all false sentences denote "the False." For Russell, too, sentences have denotations; (declarative) sentences denote propositions. Frege considered this alternative and gave an argument in favor of truth-values as the denotations of sentences. In what follows, I present Frege's argument as it is reformulated by Church in his review of Carnap's *Introduction to Semantics* (Church, [Review C], pp. 299–300), but I change it at certain points so as to free it from features peculiar to Carnap's early version of semantics. The argument applies whether or not the language contains intensional contexts, provided that it has an abstraction operator '(λx)' such that '(λx) (. . .)' means 'the class of all x such that . . .'. Let '. . .' represent a sentence, in the language S, that is true but not analytic (neither logically true nor necessarily true). Let $\mathbf{G}_1$ and $\mathbf{G}_2$ be the sentences '(λx) $(x = x . \sim \ldots) = \Lambda$' and '$\Lambda = \Lambda$' of S, respectively, where 'Λ' is a name of (λx) $(\sim x = x)$, the null class. We consider, as metalanguage for S, the language S', which is assumed to contain the whole of S and, in addition, to contain semantical terms that apply to expressions of S. In particular, S' is to contain the predicate 'Des' for designation (in S). The following are true in the metalanguage S':

(1) Des $(\mathbf{G}_1, (\lambda x)$ $(x = x . \sim \ldots) = \Lambda)$.
(2) Des $(\mathbf{G}_2, \Lambda = \Lambda)$.

Since the metalanguage S' contains the whole of the object language S, the following truth of S is also true in S':

(3) (λx) $(x = x . \sim \ldots) = \Lambda$.

Now we invoke Frege's *principle of composition,* according to which the denotation of a complex name is a function of the denotations of its constituent names. By this principle we may replace any component name, in a complex name, by any other name having the same denotation as the component name, without changing the denotation of the containing complex name. Hence from (1) and (3) we obtain

(4) Des $(\mathbf{G}_1, \Lambda = \Lambda)$.

The metalanguage is assumed to have the semantical term 'Codes' for the (binary) relation of *codesignation* (in S), which holds between any two expressions (in S) that have the same denotation. Codesignation is assumed to be an equivalence relation. From (2) and (4) we then have, as true in S',

(5)   Codes ($\mathbf{G}_1$, $\mathbf{G}_2$).

This alone suffices to establish that the designata of $\mathbf{G}_1$ and $\mathbf{G}_2$ cannot be propositions on any acceptable meaning of the term, for $\mathbf{G}_2$ is logically true in S, and $\mathbf{G}_1$ is contingent.

Of various ways of fixing a condition under which sentences are to have the same designatum, *logical equivalence* is one very natural choice for at least a sufficient condition. We will adopt this condition here. The following is a theorem of the language S'

(6)   . . . $\equiv (\lambda x) (x = x. \sim \ldots) = \Lambda$.

Hence it follows on our condition for codesignation that

(7)   . . . $= [(\lambda x) (x = x. \sim \ldots) = \Lambda]$.

We introduce $\mathbf{G}_3$ as governed by

(8)   Des ($\mathbf{G}_3$, . . .).

From (1) and (7) we obtain

(9)   Des ($\mathbf{G}_1$, . . .).

From (8) and (9) we obtain

(10)   Codes ($\mathbf{G}_1$, $\mathbf{G}_3$).

From (5) and (10), finally, we get

(11)   Codes ($\mathbf{G}_2$, $\mathbf{G}_3$).

Now $\mathbf{G}_3$ is an arbitrary contingent truth, so a like argument shows that $\mathbf{G}_2$ is codesignative with any contingent truth. But $\mathbf{G}_2$ is also codesignative with every logical truth (because it is logically equivalent to every logical truth). Hence $\mathbf{G}_2$ is codesignative with any true sentence, and consequently all true sentences are codesignative. By a similar argument, all false sentences are codesignative. The denotation of a sentence is therefore its truth-value, for nothing else will serve. This argument is not presented as conclusive but only as persuasive. There are two points at which it might be challenged. Sentences (1), (2), and (8) might be challenged because they place full sentences in positions that grammar demands be occupied by nominal expressions. For example, we would not accept

(12)   Des ('of', of)   ('of' designates of).

Designation is a binary semantical relation that holds between linguistic expressions and what they name. Hence nominal expressions must fill both blanks in 'Des (,   )'. Since designation is a semantical relation, the name to the left of the comma must be the name of a linguistic expression, and the name to the right must be the name of something that it names. In presenting his argument, Frege does assume that sentences are names, and he goes on to inquire *what* they name. He does not argue for the assumption, apparently because he regards it as not needing support. Admittedly, the assumption seems highly contentious if put in the form "Sentences are names"; but I think the only obstacle to accepting the position is terminological. What is really wrong with (12) is that 'of' lacks independent meaning. It is syncategorematic. Any categorematic expression—one having independent meaning on its own—should fit comfortably to the right of the comma in Des '(,   )'; and the full declarative sentence is the example *par excellence* of categoricity—of independent meaning.

The reluctance to accept Frege's doctrine here arises, I believe, chiefly because it is unusual to speak of sentences as "*names.*" It is not at all extraordinary, however, to treat them as names, i.e., to allow them nominal position. One treats sentences as names, i.e., as having independent meaning, as soon as one asserts that sentences "correspond to," "picture," or stand in any semantical relation whatever to something extralinguistic—to facts, states-of-affairs, or propositions. On any such view, sentences must be allowed to stand alone to the right of the comma in 'Des (,   )'.

It may seem that this consequence is avoidable. Suppose the view is that sentences "correspond to" or "describe" facts. One might then assent to the statement

Cor ('Snow is white', the fact that snow is white),

(i.e., 'Snow is white' corresponds to the fact that snow is white) but reject

Cor ('Snow is white', Snow is white),

(i.e., 'Snow is white' corresponds to Snow is white) precisely on the ground that the blank to the right of the comma in 'Cor (,   )' demands a nominal expression and sentences are not names. In response to this, I would say that the expression 'the fact that snow is white' is just an explicitly nominalized sentence. The locution 'the fact that' serves the syntactic function of transforming declarative sentences into explicit nominals where grammar demands names, but the locution has no logical or semantic significance whatever. Logically, 'the fact that snow is white' and 'Snow is white' should be accorded the same semantic analysis. From a logical point of view, we may simply dispense with the explicitly nominalizing locution 'the fact that' and treat the sentences themselves as names. The alteration effected, in our language, by this procedure would be in its *style* alone, for its logic and semantics would be unaffected.

The same remarks apply to 'the state-of-affairs that' and to 'that' itself as devices for nominalizing sentences. On any such view, sentences should be allowed to stand alone to the right of the comma in 'Des (,   )'. It would then seem hardly possible to reject (1), (2), or (8) in our argument. (If, on the other hand, the locution 'the fact that' is treated seriously as the name of a function, on the model of 'the father of', then, again, what follows 'that' must name an *argument* to the function whose value is the fact named. But 'the fact that' demands a full sentential complement, so, again, sentences are required to be treated as nominal expressions.)

There is, I have said, another point at which objection can arise. This concerns the sufficient condition for codesignation and hence the transition from step (6) to step (7) in our argument. Russell, in the first edition of *Principia Mathematica,* requires a stricter condition than logical equivalence for codesignation of sentences. But that is because he rejects the sense/reference distinction altogether and imposes an intensional interpretation on *Principia*. Let us, for the sake of this argument, accept the sense/reference distinction and inquire whether there is, within this framework, an acceptable motivation for taking logical equivalence as a sufficient condition for codesignation for sentences. Note first that, having granted the acceptability of sentences (1), (2), and (8) of our argument, we have accepted sentences as categorematic, i.e., as admissible into positions in which grammar and logic require the occurrence of nominals. We can hardly avoid the demand, then, for some criterion of codesignation; for nominals must be allowed to flank the sign of identity. Any relation between sentences that is stricter, more discriminating, than logical equivalence would seem to be a reasonable candidate as a condition for identity of sense rather than identity of reference. Three such proposals are *logical equivalence,* Carnap's *intensional isomorphism,* and Church's *synonymous isomorphism.* But these are advanced explicitly as conditions for identity of sense (intension) and not for identity of reference (extension).

We shall require that sentences, as names, obey Frege's *compositional principle* that the denotation of a complex name is a function of the denotata of its constituent names, so that the result of replacing any constituent name within a complex name by another name having the same denotation shall leave the denotation of the containing complex name unaltered. Our requirement is satisfied if we take logical equivalence as a sufficient condition of identity for the denotata of sentences. To see this, consider some cases in which the denotata of a class of complex terms are not controversial. '$(\imath x)$ (x is husband of Xanthippe . grass is green) = Socrates', is an uncontroversial truth, which remains true under substitution of logically equivalent sentences for the contained sentence, i.e., the denotation of the complex description '$(\imath x)$ (x is husband of Xanthippe . grass is green)' remains the same under such substitutions. The same is true for sentences involving abstracts such as '(λx) ($x = x$. $\sim$ . . .)', involved in our argument above. If we wish, then, to maintain the sense/reference distinction for sentences, and hence a distinction between their intension and extension, logical equivalence would seem to satisfy all our requirements for a condition for codesignation. Notice again that our argument in no way depends on the assumption that the languages under consideration are extensional languages. Hence the conclusion, if sound, holds for intensional languages as well. It follows from this that sentences having the same truth-value should be interchangeable, *salva veritate,* even in intensional contexts; but, notoriously, this is not true. Frege's way out of this contradiction consists in finding an ambiguity—namely, that sentences in intensional contexts don't denote their customary denotations, their truth-values. Ordinary languages are ambiguous. They permit the same name to have multiple senses and (hence) multiple references. There is then no failure of substitutivity, only ambiguity. Further consideration reveals that what sentences in intensional contexts denote are appropriate senses. Similar considerations lead to the conclusion that all of the logically relevant sentential parts—proper names, predicates—also are ambiguous and denote appropriate senses in intensional contexts. Since a logically perfect language excludes ambiguous expressions, it will not be constructed in accordance with the method of indirect discourse, as is ordinary language. In a language constructed in accordance with the method of direct discourse there will be no counterexamples to our conclusion that sentences denote their truth-values. From the vantage point of such a language, the purported counterexamples presented by indirect contexts in natural language are grammatical illusions, to be swept away, one and all, by disambiguation.

Historical note. I have noted that the main argument of this section for the conclusion that sentences denote their truth-values rests on the two assumptions that sentences stand in some (binary) semantical relation to extralinguistic entities and that logical equivalence is a sufficient condition for codesignation. In *Introduction to Semantics,* his first book on semantics, Carnap accepts both these assumptions but takes more finely individuated propositions rather than truth-values as denotata of sentences; as he says there, "We construe propositions in such a way that L-equivalent sentences designate the same proposition" (Carnap, [*IS*], p. 92). Carnap must have been convinced by the argument contained in Church's review of *Introduction to Semantics,* for in *Meaning and Necessity* the Fregean doctrine is accepted. Carnap might very well have taken the doctrine of *Introduction to Semantics* from Wittgenstein's *Tractatus Logico-Philosophicus* (Wittgenstein, [*TLP*]), for Wittgenstein holds, there, both that factual sentences picture facts and that logically equivalent factual sentences picture the same fact. This is central to his argument that all logical truths (tautologies) say the same thing. Contingent truths, by contrast, say different things, for they picture the vast variety of different facts that constitute "the world." The *Tractatus* avoids the conclusion that all true contingent sentences picture the same thing because it denies that logically true sentences picture anything. Without this assumption, the main argument of this section does not apply to the *Tractatus*. (See, especially, the material following (11), above.) From another point of view, this argument can be seen as a proof by contradiction that within the system of the *Tractatus* logical truths and logical contradictions are not pictures.

VI

Davidson's Criticism of Frege's Hierarchy of Senses

Donald Davidson objects to Frege's infinite hierarchy of indirect senses, and to its application to the analysis of intensional contexts, on quite different grounds from criticisms based on considerations of economy. He contends that the language that Frege describes (and, following him, Church as well) "is, even in principle, unlearnable" (Davidson, [TMLL], p. 393).

The argument that any language having the features ascribed to it by Frege (and Church) is unlearnable runs as follows. Such languages have an infinite vocabulary of semantically primitive expressions. Given some obviously correct empirical assumptions, such as that all men are mortal and that it takes some finite period of time to learn the meaning of a semantic primitive, Davidson's conclusion follows. A semantically primitive expression is one that does not contain semantically relevant parts. Thus, its sense is not a function of the senses of its constituents, for it has no constituents with sense. Consequently, the sense of each such primitive must be separately, and independently, acquired. If it is granted that the theory of Frege and Church does require such an infinite primitive vocabulary, Davidson's conclusion about unlearnability follows.

What I do not accept is Davidson's conclusion that, for this reason alone, Frege's theory of indirect discourse is unacceptable. What should be concluded is rather that, in fact, no one can completely master the Frege-Church language, for he can never know the senses of all of its words. It does not follow from this that a community of people could not master enough of the Frege-Church language for all human purposes. After all, human beings, with their limited time and memories, rarely produce or need sentences in which indirect-discourse operators are iterated more than a few times. Suppose they take the time to learn all they need. Nothing in Davidson's argument prevents our people from completely mastering the syntax of the Frege-Church language; all they lack is some far-out vocabulary. And which of us can claim to know all the words of our language? The infinite language of Frege-Church is not a naturalistic description but an idealized model of our language. Why should this model not contain features absent from the real world? The fact that the ideal-ized model contains an infinite vocabulary of primitive expressions does not entail that actual speakers must learn the senses of all of them!

In later writing, Davidson does not repeat his unlearnability argu-ment against the Frege-Church language and its infinite hierarchy of senses. In this work his argument takes a different form. Now he says that any language incorporating an infinite number of names is be-yond the competence of a Tarski-style truth-theory. A Tarski-style truth-definition recursively assigns a truth-value to all of the infinite sentences of a language, but the recursion presupposes a finite lexi-con of items (primitive constants in the category of singular terms, and predicates) each of which is separately assigned a denotation. Thus any language with an infinite lexicon, like that of Frege-Church, is beyond the reach of a Tarski-style definition of truth. And if what is wanted is not a definition of truth but a theory that takes *truth* as a primitive concept, to be characterized by axioms, then, if the primitive vocabulary is infinite, the axioms are also required to be infinite, since the primitive terms each require separate character-ization. In this form, Davidson's criticism is that the language of Frege-Church is beyond the reach of a finite truth-theory. Now if a theory of meaning for a language is taken to be (or to include) a theory of truth for the language, and if to learn a language is taken to consist in mastering (implicitly) a theory of meaning for it, then any language with an infinite vocabulary is unlearnable in its totality.

I would reply to this form of Davidson's criticism again, as above, that the language system with infinite axioms is not, after all, presented as a naturalistic description of our language but as an idealized model that attempts to explain the essential mechanisms that underlie its working. It need never be claimed that the infinite language is a possible human language. Even if it is granted that it is not, it still remains that it may provide the best account available of actual language. Nevertheless, on grounds of economy, I would propose the adoption of the following simple alternative compromise between the infinite languages of Frege-Church and the complete elimination of indirect senses proposed by Dummett. In accordance with the method of indirect discourse, we recognize for each name just its customary sense, its customary reference, its oblique (indirect) sense, and its indirect reference, which is the same as its customary sense. If we follow, rather, the method of direct discourse in the treatment of oblique contexts, we adopt a new (notationally related) sign to replace the name in oblique contexts. The same replacement is used no matter how many indirect-discourse operators the context containing the name contains. This simple compromise has the following advantages: (1) It is not subject to Davidson's unlearnability argument, since the vocabulary is finite. (2) For the same reason, it is amenable to a Tarski-style truth-definition and to a finite truth-theory. (3) It accounts, as well as the infinite languages account, for failure of substitutivity in oblique contexts. (Note that this proposal does not abandon, in the method of indirect discourse, the infinite hierarchy of senses but only the infinite hierarchy of indirect senses. Again, in the method of direct discourse, it abandons the infinite hierarchy of names but not the infinite hierarchy of senses.) (4) It has the advantage over Dummett's proposal of preserving the basic principle that sense and sense alone determines reference. The alternative, I advocate, can be applied as well, in a straightforward way, to the representation of indirect discourse (and intensional contexts generally) in a formalized language using the method of direct discourse. Here we have, instead of an infinite hierarchy of names associated with each name, only one other name, say 'N_1', associated with each name 'N'. In this form of the theory, 'N_1' denotes the customary sense of 'N' and consequently has a different sense than 'N'.

The theory I advocate is a two-level theory as opposed to Frege's assumed infinite-level theory. I recommend it, however, solely on the grounds of conceptual economy, not because I accept Davidson's contention that a Tarski-style truth-definition cannot be provided for the infinite-level form of the theory advocated by Frege. Davidson's argument rests on the following assumption: The infinite sequence of different senses of higher degrees associated with each name cannot be predicted (generated) recursively, i.e., it cannot be generated constructively. This is not at all evident, and, in fact, it is not true. Let 'N' be an arbitrary name and let '$N_|$' be its *first ascendant*. The first ascendant of a name 'N' denotes the sense of 'N'; similarly, the second ascendant of 'N', viz., '$N_{||}$' denotes the sense of the first ascendant '$N_|$' of 'N', and so on *ad infinitum*. Now this rule recursively generates a denotation for each of the infinitely many ascendants of the name 'N'. To see this, observe that 'N', by assumption, already has a sense and a reference. Now the sense of 'N' becomes, by our rule, the reference of '$N_|$'. My claim is that our rule thus also implicitly assigns a sense to '$N_|$', and this sense in turn becomes the reference of '$N_{||}$'. The sense that our rule assigns can perhaps be expressed by this paraphrase: the reference of a name is the sense of that name that is its *immediate descendant,* where 'N' with $n - 1$ strokes in its subscript is the immediate descendant of the name 'N' with n strokes in its subscript. This rule applies as long as $n \geq 1$. For $n = 0$, the sense and reference of the name are given outright in the basis clause of the recursion. The principle to which I am appealing is that, since the rule determines reference, it thereby determines sense. This is Frege's principle that sense and sense alone determines reference.

The two-level theory I advocate introduces one level of indirect sense. By the argument of section III, however, I am committed to an infinite hierarchy of direct senses. If every direct sense is required to have a name, the infinite hierarchy of names is required as well.

4

Russell's Theory of
Oblique Contexts

I

(1) Scott is the author of *Waverley*. (2) George IV wished to know whether Scott was the author of *Waverley*. Therefore, (3) George IV wished to know whether Scott was Scott. Why does this conclusion not follow from the premises? Russell introduces this puzzle in "On Denoting" as one of three puzzles that he says a theory of denoting ought to be able to solve. He says of the puzzles, "I shall show that my theory solves them" (Russell, [OD], p. 47; subsequent parenthetical page references are to this source). Russell accepts the principle of substitutivity—to which we appeal, in passing, to the conclusion from the premises—but he holds the argument to be only apparently sanctioned by it. He formulates this principle as follows: "If *a* is identical with *b,* whatever is true of the one is true of the other, and either may be substituted for the other in any proposition without altering the truth or falsehood of that proposition" (p. 47). Such formulations are often taken to illustrate Russell's pervasive insensitivity to the distinction between use and mention. But if we recall that, for Russell, the referent of a name is itself a constituent of the proposition in whose "verbal expression" the name occurs, such passages as the one just quoted can be seen to have a entirely clear interpretation, not involving use/mention confusion at all.

I will call the puzzle stated in the beginning of the last paragraph "Russell's puzzle," but the name is not historically accurate. Of course the specific form given the puzzle is due to Russell, but essentially the same problem is discussed at length by Frege, both in "On Sense and Reference" and in his correspondence, and in chapter 3 I discussed Frege's treatment of it. Note how close Russell's puzzle is to Frege's puzzle about identity. Frege's puzzle asks, "How can

'Scott is the author of *Waverley*' differ in cognitive value from 'Scott is Scott', provided the former is true?." Russell's question—how George IV could have wished to know the former but not the latter—is just the question how the two statements of identity can differ in cognitive value for George IV, provided the former of them is true.

When we rewrite premises (1) and (2) in accordance with Russell's theory, the definite description "disappears on analysis." Thus there is no definite description in (the analyzed version of) (2) to be replaced by 'Scott'. The puzzle, according to this theory, is produced by a logical mirage. This is Russell's solution. "The puzzle about George IV's curiosity is now seen to have a very simple solution. The proposition 'Scott was the author of *Waverley*', which was written out in its unabbreviated form in the preceding paragraph, does not contain any constituent 'the author of *Waverley*' for which we could substitute 'Scott' " (pp. 51–52). Here, I think, one can complain of a tendency to slide over the use/mention distinction, but the sense is clear. When Russell writes of the "proposition . . . which was written out in the preceding paragraph," he must be understood to be referring to sentence (1), i.e., to the "verbal expression" of the proposition cited. Thus understood, Russell is saying that, correctly analyzed, the proposition expressed by sentence (1) does not authorize the substitution in (2) that leads to the false conclusion (3). The reason is that, according to Russell's theory, (1) does not express an identity at all, since the description "disappears on analysis." I assume that Russell meant this and that it is to this substitution that he objects.

II

The "solution" is inadequate. The premises contain no definite description after it has been eliminated in accordance with Russell's analysis. But it does not follow from this consideration that the propositions (1), (2), and (3), when thus analyzed, do not constitute a valid argument. After all, we may, under some conditions, validly substitute proper names for definite descriptions in the "verbal expressions" of propositions containing them. There is a theorem of *Principia* to this effect:

*14.15 $\{(\imath x)(\phi x) = b\} \supset \{(\psi(\imath x)(\phi x)) \equiv (\psi b)\}$.

Indeed, the fundamental intuition behind Russell's theory of descriptions is that, although these expressions masquerade as genuine singular terms, from a logical point of view they are not genuine singular terms. The theorem *14.15 is the most important formal expression of this intuition; for descriptions can be interpreted as playing the role of genuine singular terms only because they may replace and be replaced by genuine names under certain conditions. Logically that is what the "masquerade" (Bentham wrote of "fictions") consists in. Thus, on any acceptable account of definite descriptions, they must behave in accordance with *14.15. Of course names and descriptions cannot in all respects behave alike; if they did, it would not be an illusion that they are names, for they would then indeed be names. The incompleteness of these symbols must manifest itself (be "relevant," Russell says) somehow.

What is wrong with the view under consideration is that the descriptive phrase is required, as Russell says, to have "primary occurrence" in both of its occurrences in *14.15, but it has primary occurrence only in the first premiss of the argument formulated in (1), (2), and (3). What Russell tells us now (pp. 51–52) is that, in any proposition in whose verbal expression 'the author of *Waverley*' has a primary occurrence, we may validly replace it by 'Scott' (assuming (1), of course). But then it appears that Russell has abandoned the logical-mirage theory in the very paragraph in which he presents it. Now he leaves us to suppose that what is wrong with replacing 'the author of *Waverley*' by 'Scott' in (2) on the basis of (1) is that the description does not have a primary occurrence in (2).

III

Russell does not tell us why the interpretation of premiss (2) that finds in it a primary occurrence of the description (hereafter I call this "the primary interpretation") is wrong. But it is wrong; for (2) on this interpretation entails that *Waverley* was not coauthored. If *Waverley* had been coauthored, it would not, on the primary interpretation, be logically possible that George IV should have wished to know whether Scott was the author of *Waverley.* But no plausible analysis of our proposition can have this as a consequence. A sufficient condition for the truth of (2) is that George IV should have asked, in all seriousness, "Is Scott the author of *Waverley?*" Now surely he might seriously have asked this question even if *Waverley* had been coauthored. What is the proof that the unwanted consequence follows on the primary interpretation of (2)? On this interpretation, (2) is of the form:

(4) $(\exists c)\{((\phi x) \equiv_x (x = c)) . (\psi c)\}.$

Simplifying by eliminating the right conjunct, we get:

(5) $(\exists c)\{(\phi x) \equiv_x (x = c)\}.$

This, by the definition *14.02 of *Principia,* is the definitional expansion of

(6) $E!\ (\imath x)(\phi x).$

Consistently with the interpretation we have supplied for the variables above, this says,

(7)   One and only one person wrote *Waverley.*

And (7) entails that *Waverley* was not coauthored. (This argument is taken from my paper "Reference and Referents" [RR]).

This result brings out in a particularly revealing way what it is that the primary interpretation misses. It misses the feature of (2) that makes it "intentional" in the technical sense. "Intentional" verbs behave in a characteristic way as concerns the existence of their objects. It is not possible to take a bath in a nonexistent tub. But it is possible for someone to want to take a bath in my tub even though I do not, in fact, possess one. Just so, George IV could not have assaulted the author of *Waverley* if *Waverley* had been coauthored, but he could have wanted to know whether Scott was the author of *Waverley* if *Waverley* had been coauthored and even if no such book as *Waverley* had ever been written. Thus the primary interpretation of

(2) is not correct, and we escape the conclusion that (1) (2) (3) is a valid argument.

We turn then to the alternative interpretation that Russell's theory provides for (2)—the "secondary interpretation." (2) now is taken to be of the form

$$(8) \quad \chi \left\{ \left[(\imath x)(\phi x) \right] \psi(\imath x)(\phi x) \right\}.$$

The sign '$[(\imath x)(\phi x)]$' in (8) is Russell's "scope operator," and in this formula it indicates that the descriptive phrase is to be eliminated from the subordinate clause '$\psi(\imath x) (\phi x)$' and not from the whole of (8). That is, the result of eliminating the description from (8) is

$$(9) \quad \chi \left\{ (\exists c)(\{(\phi x) \equiv_x (x = c)\} \cdot \{\psi c\}) \right\}.$$

An English sentence that might be translated into (9) would be:

(10)   George IV wished to know whether one and only one person wrote *Waverley* and that person was Scott.

What happens to (2) on the secondary analysis is just that the "intentional" expression 'George IV wished to know whether' is isolated by the scope operator from the subordinate clause from which the descriptive phrase is to be eliminated. The description is then eliminated from this subordinate clause. There is really just one analysis of propositions of the form $\psi(\imath x) (\phi x)$, and this is given by definition *14.01. The difference between the primary and secondary interpretations, as I have been calling them, is determined by the part of (2) (proper or improper) taken as $\psi(\imath x) (\phi x)$. On the secondary interpretation, $\psi(\imath x) (\phi x)$ is taken to be not the whole of (2) but the part

(11)   Scott is the author of *Waverley*.

Though we have but one analysis of $\psi(\imath x) (\phi x)$, we have two (non-equivalent) analyses of (2), according as we take the whole of (2) or the part (11) as $\psi(\imath x) (\phi x)$.

IV

Under the secondary interpretation, (2) is represented as having the form (8). When (2) is given this interpretation, (1) (2) (3) constitutes a valid argument if and only if the following conditional is valid:

$$(15) \quad \{a = (\imath x)(\phi x)\} \supset \{(\chi\{[(\imath x)(\phi x)]\psi(\imath x)(\phi x)\}) \supset (\chi\{\psi a\})\}.$$

In the final paragraph of chapter 14 of *Principia* Russell says, "It should be observed that the proposition in which $(\imath x)$ (ϕx) has the larger scope always implies the corresponding one in which it has the smaller scope, but the converse implication holds only if either (a) we have $E!(\imath x)$ (ϕx) or (b) the proposition in which $(\imath x)$ (ϕx) has the smaller scope implies $E!(\imath x)$ (ϕx)." Part of what Russell is here telling us is put formally thus:

$$(16) \quad \{E!(\imath x)(\phi x)\} \supset \{(\chi[(\imath x)(\phi x]\psi(\imath x)(\phi x)) \equiv ([(\imath x)(\phi x)] \chi \{\psi(\imath x)(\phi x)\})\}.$$

Now, if this is true, the interpretation that accords a secondary occurrence to 'the author of *Waverley*' in (2) yields an argument (call it "1′2′3′") that is valid. This can be shown as follows. (1) (2) (3) is valid when the descriptive phrase is accorded a primary occurrence in (2); i.e., the following is valid by *14.15:

1. $a = (\imath x)$ (ϕx),
2. $\chi\{\psi(\imath x)(\phi x)\}$,
∴ 3. $\chi(\psi a)$.

What we want to show is that the following argument that accords a secondary occurrence to the description is also valid:

1′. $a = (\imath x)$ (ϕx),
2′. $\chi\{[(\imath x)(\phi x)]\psi(\imath x)(\phi x)\}$,
∴ 3′. $\chi(\psi a)$.

Now, it is valid; for from 1′ follows 4′: $E!(\imath x)$ (ϕx) (by *14.21). By assumption, we have 5′, i.e., (16). From 4′ and 5′ we get

74

6'. $\{\chi[(\imath x)(\phi x)] \; \psi(\imath x)(\phi x)\} \equiv \{[(\imath x)(\phi x)] \; \chi(\psi(\imath x)(\phi x))\}$.

Now, by 2' and 6', we get

7'. $[(\imath x)(\phi x)] \; \chi \; \{\psi(\imath x)(\phi x)\}$.

But 7' = 2, and 1' = 1; hence, since 1 2 3 is valid and 3' = 3, it follows that 1'2'3' is valid.

Russell thought the argument (1) (2) (3), under the interpretation according secondary occurrence to the description in (2), invalid; and so it is. The source of the difficulty is that (16) is not true. We have just shown that. Russell says in at least three places in *Principia* that (16) is true. In the introduction he says, "It will be seen further that when E!$(\imath x)$ (ϕx), we may enlarge or diminish the scope of $(\imath x)$ (ϕx) as much as we please without altering the truth-value of any proposition in which it occurs" (p. 70). Again, at the end of chapter 14 he says, "The purpose of the following propositions is to show that, when E!$(\imath x)$ (ϕx), the scope of $(\imath x)$ (ϕx) does not matter to the truth-value of any proposition in which $(\imath x)$ (ϕx) occurs. This proposition cannot be proved generally, but it can be proved in each particular case." We are then given a series of theorems (*14.31–34) in which it is proved that, when $(\imath x)$ (ϕx) occurs in the form $\chi(\imath x)$ (ϕx) and $\chi(\imath x)$ (ϕx) occurs in turn as part of a larger proposition, the scope of $(\imath x)$ (ϕx) does not affect the truth-value of the larger proposition, provided E!$(\imath x)$ (ϕx).

Now, of course, there is no reason to believe that Russell was really unaware of any of this. Although he *says* that when E!$(\imath x)$ (ϕx), "we may enlarge or diminish the scope of $(\imath x)$ (ϕx) as much as we please without altering the truth-value of any proposition in which it occurs" (p. 70) and makes other remarks to the same effect in other passages, he also, in the following passage, describes the situation correctly: "The purpose of the following propositions is to show that, when E!$(\imath x)$ (ϕx), the scope of $(\imath x)$ (ϕx) does not matter to the truth-value of any proposition in which $(\imath x)$ (ϕx) occurs. . . . The proposition can be proved generally when $(\imath x)$ (ϕx) occurs in the form χ $(\imath x)$ (ϕx) and χ $(\imath x)$ (ϕx) occurs in what we may call a 'truth function', i.e. a function whose truth or falsehood depends only upon the truth or falsehood of its argument or arguments" (p. 184). The proposition cannot be "proved generally," he says, and we must take him to mean that that is because it is not true generally but only for extensional contexts. The proposition that can be "proved generally" is the theorem *14.3, in which the antecedent condition,

$$\{(p \equiv q) \supset_{p, q} (f(p) \equiv f(q))\} \; . \; E!(\imath x)(\phi x),$$

is clearly meant, as the above remark of Russell makes clear, to restrict the scope of the theorem to proper descriptions in extensional contexts. But *14.3 cannot then be used, as (16) was, to establish the validity of 1' 2' 3', because 2' is a nonextensional context. In theorem *14.3, with its implied restrictions, is expressed the most fundamental observation concerning intensional contexts that is associated with Russell's theory of descriptions.

In presenting formulas such as (9) and 2' as representing possible alternative Russellian analysis of 'George IV wished to know whether Scott was the author of *Waverley*', we cannot claim the explicit authority of Russell. Russell, of course, discusses the alternative analyses that I have called "primary" and "secondary," but his discussion is always informal; he never presents the alternatives in the notation of *Principia Mathematica*, and indeed there is a serious difficulty in the way of doing this. *Principia* was designed, in the first place, to provide an account of the language and foundations of mathematics. For this reason, any formal account of statements of assertion and belief could safely be left out of that work. But the difficulty is this: Church has observed that, although formation rules for *Principia Mathematica* are not fully and clearly stated, it is nevertheless, apparently, the intention of the authors that the argument-expressions of a functional variable or a functional constant (if such are to be added to the system) are to be variables or primitive constants only and not more complex formulas (Church, [RSTT], pp. 27–28). Church observes that there are several passages in which the authors of *Principia* clearly presuppose the reducibility of all well-formed formulas to prenex form (see especially *12), although the requirement is never explicitly stated. The rule restricting argument-expressions for propositional-functional symbols is violated in some informal discursive passages (and even in the formulation of theorem *14.3). Nevertheless, it does seem clear that the reducibility requirement is intended. Now, under this restriction, formulas such as (9), 2, and 2′, which have played such a central role in the above account, are simply not well formed. Indeed, under this restriction, there would seem to be no way of formulating such statements as 'George IV believes that Scott = the author of *Waverley,*' in its alternative interpretations, primary and secondary, in *Principia Mathematica.* What my formulas should be understood to represent, then, are formulations of my paradigm sentences into a *Principia*-like notation not constrained by the requirement of reducibility to prenex form. These formulations are suggested by Russell's informal discussions of these topics, but my formulations are not to be taken as belonging to *Principia* itself (even with the addition of primitive constants).

V

What then is Russell's solution to his puzzle? The argument (1) (2) (3) has the surface-grammatical form of a simple inference by substitutivity of identity. But the surface grammar of (2) is misleading as to its underlying logical form, which is correctly represented by (9). Now the logical-mirage account finally assumes its proper place; for examination of (9) reveals no definite description to be replaced by an appeal to the law of the substitutivity of identity. At the same time, the argument (1) (2) (3) is not licensed by theorem *14.15, because the definite description in *14.15 has a primary occurrence, while the description in (2) has a secondary occurrence. So the correct logical form of (1) (2) (3) is given by 1′ 2′ 3′, above. This is an invalid argument. Furthermore, it does not reduce to the form *14.15 in virtue of *14.3, which establishes that distinctions of scope for proper (denoting) descriptions can be ignored in extensional contexts; for 2′ contains the description in an intensional context. Finally, the Russellian solution to the puzzle isolates the fallacy that produces it as consisting in ignoring the intensional character of premiss (2). If we call a description $(\imath x) (\phi x)$ a "proper" description just in case E! $(\imath x) (\phi x)$, then the positive lesson to be learned from this solution to Russell's puzzle is this: *Any sentence containing even a proper definite description has nonequivalent interpretations depending on the scope accorded the description, provided the sentence expresses an intensional context.* To accept the argument (1) (2) (3) as valid because it is of the form *14.15 is, on Russell's account, a fallacy of ambiguity. The fallacy is one of ambiguity according to Frege's theory as well, except that, according to him, the ambiguity is lexical—i.e., the words 'the author of *Waverley*' in (2) denote their oblique reference, not their customary reference. Hence the identity (1), in which these same words denote their customary reference, does not authorize the substitution made to arrive at the false conclusion (3). Russell's ambiguity is, by contrast, not lexical but structural or syntactic. The premiss (2) has two underlying logical forms, and these are not equivalent. In the terminology of older logic texts, the inference from (1) and (2) to (3) is a fallacy of amphiboly.

Let us now consider another form of Russell's puzzle, involving the premisses

A. The author of *Waverley* = the author of *Ivanhoe*.
B. George IV wishes to know whether the author of *Waverley* = the author of *Ivanhoe*.

Therefore,

C. George IV wishes to know whether the author of *Waverley* = the author of *Waverley*.

One could then repeat Russell's remark concerning C, that an interest in the law of identity can hardly be attributed to the first gentleman of Europe.

The reason for considering this slightly different form of Russell's puzzle is this: The Russellian analysis of B and C produces propositions that differ in truth-value. The only difference between B and C is that the former contains the description 'the author of *Ivanhoe*' and the latter does not. In their analyzed form B and C differ only in that the analyzed form of B contains an expression denoting the propositional function *x authors Ivanhoe* where the analyzed form of C contains an expression denoting the propositional function *x authors Waverley*. These propositional functions are identical in extension, assuming that A is true. If B and C are to differ in truth-value, it follows that these propositional functions must be intensional and not extensional entities. For purposes of Russell's solution to his puzzle, propositional functions must be interpreted intensionally and not extensionally.

Russell's solution to his puzzle requires that the entities denoted in sentences with descriptions be intensional entities that he calls "propositional functions." More precisely, they must be the propositional functions denoted by the predicates in the contained definite descriptions, since the descriptions as a whole are incomplete symbols, which denote nothing. Thus, intensional sentences such as (2) and B come to express relations between intensions. Further, the propositional functions denoted are, in the cases I am considering here, uniquely satisfied. They are what Russell calls "unitary" propositional functions.

This way of putting the matter brings Russell's solution to his puzzle very close to Frege's solution to the same puzzle. For Frege, descriptions in oblique contexts, such as (2) and B denote their customary sense. The sense expressed by any name is a concept of at most one object (in the case of denoting names, of exactly one object). Hence the sense of a proper name is remarkably similar to Russell's unitary propositional function.

Let us further compare the analysis of intentional idioms supplied by the theories of Russell and Frege. We have seen that whereas Frege's account turns on the contention of reference shift—in oblique contexts names denote their customary sense—Russell's account turns on scope ambiguities. It would seem, then, that the Russellian account must face some difficulty in the case of intentional idioms that are not productive of the sentential complements needed for ambiguities of scope to occur. Consider the example [Church]

Ponce de Leon sought the fountain of youth.

Since 'sought' does not take a sentential complement, we cannot invoke the scope distinctions that Russell deploys for the analysis of intensional contexts. If we treat 'the fountain of youth' as a description, Russell's theory leaves us no alternative but the primary analysis, and this must be rejected because of the existential entailment required by that analysis. On the primary analysis, our sentence is *false*, not true, as it should be on any acceptable account.

The Fregean treatment, by contrast, has rather smooth sailing. According to this, 'sought' induces an oblique context, and in our sentence 'the fountain of youth' denotes its customary sense. The sentence, then, expresses a relation between Ponce de Leon and a sense—a relation that, as Church remarks, is not quite that of *seeking*.

The Russellian treatment requires that the 'sought-for' idiom be replaced by one that demands the needed sentential complement. The following will perhaps do:

Ponce de Leon sought to bring it about that Ponce de Leon should find the fountain of youth.

The Russellian analysis can now accord a secondary occurrence to the contained description. This account presupposes the synonymy of this sentence and our original sentence about Ponce de Leon, and it might well be rejected for that reason.

Another type of case that *prima facie* is not amenable to the Russellian account is presented by the following sentence:

Lady Hamilton is like in beauty to Aphrodite. [Church]

On the Fregean account, this sentence is without truth-value because it contains a denotationless name. On the Russellian account 'Aphrodite' is a truncated description, perhaps 'the aphroditizer'; and, because of the absence of a sentential complement, it can be interpreted only as false. There is here, I believe, little to choose between the Fregean and Russellian solutions. The one treatment assigns our sentence no truth-value; the other judges it false. I have some inclination to regard it as true, but the intuition is not all that strong. Let the decision be determined by the further decision as to which theory enjoys overall superiority!

There is another case like this, except that it is undoubtedly true:

Homer worshiped Zeus.

On the Fregean account, our conviction that this is true must carry over to a conviction that 'worship' induces an oblique context. Here

80

'Zeus' denotes its customary sense. The required Russellian account is more difficult to come by. 'Zeus' must be treated as a disguised description, 'the zeusizer'. But again we face the problem of the missing sentential complement, without which our sentence becomes false on the Russellian account. This is like several other puzzle-sentences that Church, who is the source of many of these puzzles (Church, [NAESA], p. 442), also considers: "I am thinking of Pegasus," "Barbara Villiers was less chaste than Diana." Any proposal to treat 'Pegasus' in the first of these as a description, e.g., as 'the pegasizer', runs up against the consideration that it gives the sentence being considered the wrong truth-value. He then says, "For the Russell theory it might be suggested to analyze them as being about the property of being a Pegasus, the property of being a fountain of youth, and the property of being a Diana" (Church, ibid.). This brings the Russellian treatment of these cases very close to the Fregean, and both seem intuitively quite satisfactory. But, as Church points out, this analysis again introduces names of properties, and, on pain of reintroducing Frege's paradox of identity, these names of properties must themselves be capable of elimination by contextual definition, unless the vocabulary of the language is so severely restricted as to prohibit alternative names for properties that are not synonymous. Chapter 2 contains a discussion of this last topic.

5

Doxastic Logic

This chapter and the two that follow deal with some alternative (and rival) solutions to those offered by Frege and Russell for the central problems connected with oblique contexts. I will also consider some criticisms of the classical theories of Frege and Russell. One alternative is to be found in the possible-worlds semantics for modality, which has received so much study recently. This is the topic of the present chapter.

I

The syntactic and semantic analogies between statements of propositional attitude, on the one hand, and statements of necessity, contingency, possibility, and impossibility, on the other, are so close that it is logical to classify them together, with the latter group set apart as the modalities of truth—the "alethic" modalities. 'Knows that . . .' and 'believes that . . .', like 'It is necessary that . . .' and 'It is possible that . . .', are, like 'It is not the case that . . .', singulary connectives that, when applied to statements, produce more complex statements. Unlike the results involving negation, however, the others are nontruth-functional. They reject the principle of the substitutivity of identity, according to which the two terms of a true identity-statement are everywhere intersubstitutive, *salva veritate,* and they involve problems of interpretation when a contained variable is bound by an initial quantifier.

In accordance with suggestions made by Leibniz, statements of alethic modality may be translated into others about possible worlds. 'It is necessary that p' is paraphrased as 'In all possible worlds, it is the case that p', and 'It is possible that p' is paraphrased as 'In at least one possible world, it is the case that *p*'. No one, I suppose, believes that these paraphrases about possible worlds constitute an analysis, explanation, or clarification of statements of alethic modality. If you do not understand the statement that it is necessary that *p*, it won't help to be told that it means that *p* is the case in all possible worlds. The order of explanation goes rather in the other direction. Any way that one might devise to explain what it means to say that there is a possible world in which it is the case that *p* will say nothing more than that it might have been the case that *p*.

There are those who claim that assertions of what might have been, counterfactual statements, and statements in the subjunctive mood generally are beyond the bounds of clear sense. They will, of course, not be helped by paraphrasing the suspect statements into others about possible worlds. These, they will say, are as much in need of explanation as the counterfactual subjunctives with which we started. And they will be right to say this. Statements about possible worlds are as much in need of explanation as the statements in the subjunctive mood that they translate. But no more so. So, those of us who are fortunate enough to understand the subjunctive mood face no additional difficulties over possible worlds.

What is gained by the paraphrase? It is a device for translating the subjunctive into the indicative mood. 'You might have been hit by that car' becomes 'There is a possible world in which you are hit by that car'. The latter gives the truth-conditions of the former, and it points the way to the formal semantics of modality. Since Skolem we have known how to construct the model-theoretic semantics of part of our indicative discourse. This part includes all of classical mathematics. The possible-worlds semantics of modality extends this to areas of the subjunctive by reducing them to the indicative mood, keeping close to the classical model.

Possible-worlds semantics deals so successfully with alethic modalities that it is natural to suppose that the same approach to the propositional attitudes will be successful, in view of the close semantic and syntactic analogies between them. The guiding intuition is clear. Consider the parallel cases of knowledge and belief. To say that the person *a* knows (believes) that *p* is to invoke the idea of a set of "epistemically" ("doxastically") possible worlds (with respect to the person *a*) in which it is the case that *p*. Everything that *a* knows (believes) is true in each of these worlds. These worlds are all compatible with what he knows (believes), though they generally differ in ways that make them incompatible with each other.

It is a's task, as a rational agent, to plan his projects and to act in accordance with his knowledge and beliefs as to how the world really is. But any agent has a very limited stock of knowledge, and his positive beliefs do not extend very far either. There is a lot he does not know or even have beliefs about. In conducting his affairs he needs to consider lots of different ways the world might be—ways that are each compatible with what he knows or believes it really is, though perhaps they are incompatible with each other. There are lots of possible worlds he need not consider at all. They are incompatible with what he knows or believes. These intuitions lead to the following principles:

> a knows (believes) that p if, and only if, in every epistemically (doxastically) possible world compatible with what a knows (believes) it is the case that p.

> a does not know (believe) that p if, and only if, in some epistemically (doxastically) possible world compatible with what a knows (believes) it is not the case that p.

So far we have considered 'knows that . . .' and 'believes that . . .'. An equally important idiom is 'knows who . . .'. Hintikka represents 'a knows who b is' as $(\exists x) K_a (x = b)$, where $(\exists x) B_a (x = b)$ represents the corresponding doxastic notion. For the alethic modalities there is no corresponding locution in our ordinary idiom, but the formula

$$(\exists x) \square (x = b)$$

expresses a very important notion, which may be translated, by semantic ascent, as ' 'b' denotes the same thing in every possible world', i.e., 'b' is a rigid designator. Here is another important analogy between the two classes of modal concepts. 'b' 's being a rigid designator has its epistemic analogue in a's knowing who b is. Thus, to say that a knows who b is, is to say that 'b' denotes the same individual in all (epistemically) possible worlds (with respect to a); i.e., it says that 'b' is an epistemically rigid designator. Similarly, $(\exists x) \, B_a \, (x = b)$ says that 'b' denotes the same individual in all doxastically possible worlds (with respect to a); i.e., it says that 'b' is a doxastically rigid designator.

These analogies are so smooth and convincing that the dis-analogies between the two great classes of modal concepts have tended to drop out of sight. This is unfortunate because, in fact, these analogies, strong as they are, are misleading. In the remainder of this chapter I will indicate where they fail.

II

In my note "On Interpreting Doxastic Logic" (Linsky, [IDL]) it was shown that the concept of defensibility formalized in Jaakko Hintikka's doxastic logic was incorrectly characterized by him in his informal accounts in *Knowledge and Belief* (Hintikka, [*KB*]). There Hintikka explains that his notion of defensibility amounts to "immunity to certain kinds of criticism." For Hintikka, to say that a statement of belief or a knowledge-claim is "indefensible" is to say that its maker is guilty of a lack of logical acumen in that he has failed to follow up the logical consequences of what he knows or believes ([*KB*], p. 31).

In my note, I showed that Hintikka's account is inadequate in the case of the statement "$B_b B_c p$," where 'p' represents an inconsistent statement (in the sense of standard first-order predicate logic), and 'b' and 'c' name different persons. The indefensibility of the statement is proved by the following argument, where μ^* is a doxastic alternative to μ (with respect to b), μ^{**} is a doxastic alternative to μ^* (with respect to c), and 'p' contains no epistemic or doxastic operators. (My use of double quotation marks around formulas adheres to Hintikka's conventions [see [*KB*], p. 4]. A list of conditions on model sets cited in proofs is given at the end of the chapter.)

$$(1) \quad \text{``}B_b B_c p\text{''} \epsilon \mu \qquad \text{counterassumption}$$
$$(2) \quad \text{``}B_c p\text{''} \epsilon \mu^* \qquad \text{from (1) and (C.b*)}$$
$$(3) \quad p \epsilon \mu^{**} \qquad \text{from (2) and (C.b*)}$$

Intuitively, model sets are (partial) descriptions of possible worlds and are defined by a set of conditions that have the following property:

> If we disregard epistemic notions, the resulting system may be shown to be equivalent to the usual formulations of quantification theory in the sense that a formula is valid (self-sustaining) if and only if it is provable in the usual formulations. (Strictly speaking, we have to use a formulation in which empty universes of discourse are not disregarded. . . . [Hintikka, [*KB*], pp., 127–28]

This statement I shall call "Hintikka's Theorem." To say that a formula is self-sustaining is equivalent to saying that its negation is not embeddable in a model set. By Hintikka's Theorem, a formula of quantification theory is provable, and hence valid in the usual formulations, if and only if its negation is not embeddable in a model set. The relevance of these observations to the little argument begun above is this: 'p' is assumed to be an invalid sentence (in the sense of standard quantification theory). It follows from this, by Hintikka's Theorem, that, contrary to (3) above, 'p' is not a member of any model set. Hence the counterassumption (1) is refuted. Hence "$B_b B_c p$" is shown to be indefensible; it is not embeddable in a model set. The same considerations show that "$B_c p$" is indefensible as well. It follows from similar arguments that the person referred to by 'c' believes all logical truths and that he does not believe the negation of any logical truth. The conclusion to be drawn from this is that the sentences of epistemic or doxastic logic are self-sustaining (valid) only under the idealized circumstance that the knowers and believers referred to in these sentences are logically omniscient: they know and believe all logical truths, and they know and believe all of the logical consequences of what they know or believe.

What induces this idealization, in the possible-worlds account of propositional attitudes, is the fact recorded in Hintikka's Theorem that the possible-worlds account of knowledge and belief, as of all modal concepts, is a conservative extension of standard quantification theory. There is no way of avoiding the requirement of logical omniscience so long as the logic of knowledge and belief is treated within this framework. In the case of the alethic modalities, the corresponding result is entirely expected and unproblematic. What is logically true may not, in fact, be known or believed, but it is necessarily true and hence true in every possible world. What is logically inconsistent may, in fact, be believed, but it is necessarily false and hence false in every possible world, alethic, epistemic, or doxastic. With alethic modalities, no idealization is involved.

The possible-worlds analysis of propositional attitudes induces more idealization than that involved in the requirement of logical omniscience. Consider again our sentence "$B_b B_c p$", which we have proved to be indefensible whenever 'p' represents a logically inconsistent sentence. Let us assume that the idealized condition of logical omniscience obtains, so that in fact "$B_c p$" is false. Then "$B_b B_c p$" may be true even supposing both b and c to be logically omniscient. Hence our sentence is true even though neither b nor c is guilty of a failure in logical acumen: not the person c, for, by assumption, he does *not* believe p; and, again, not the person b, for although he believes that the person c has failed in logical acumen, that is a belief he is entitled to have without being open to the charge of logical density on his own part. It is not a logical truth that nobody believes a logical falsehood. So, in this case, no one is guilty of logical density. This result shows that Hintikka's formal conditions on model sets do not formalize the intuitive notion that he characterizes in *Knowledge and Belief,* which he there calls "virtual belief."

Kathleen G. Johnson Wu, in "Hintikka and Defensibility," has extended my result to Hintikka's epistemic logic as well (Wu, [HD]). The failure of Hintikka's epistemic logic to adequately formalize the intuitive notion he characterizes as "virtual knowledge" is there established by demonstration of a number of counterexamples. For this case we need a sentence that (1) is indefensible according to the logic, i.e., it is not embeddable in a model set, and (2) is defensible according to the informal account of that notion already given. We may take the sentence "$B_b B_c p$", which we have already shown to satisfy these requirements. Now let us consider the following epistemic sentence "$\sim K_a \sim B_b B_c p$", where 'p' again represents an inconsistent sentence of standard quantification theory. The following is Wu's demonstration of the indefensibility of this sentence in epistemic logic. Assume for some model system Ω and for some model set $\mu \epsilon \Omega$

(4) "$\sim K_a \sim B_b B_c p$"$\epsilon \mu$ counterassumption
(5) "$P_a \sim \sim B_b B_c p$"$\epsilon \mu$ from (4), (C.$\sim$K)
(6) "$\sim \sim B_b B_c p$"$\epsilon \mu *$ 5, (C.P*)
(7) "$B_b B_c p$"$\epsilon \mu *$ 6, (C.$\sim\sim$)

By our earlier argument we have already established the negation of (7). Hence our counterassumption is refuted, and the sentence "$K_a \sim B_b B_c p$" ('p' inconsistent) is proved self-sustaining. Now, once again, (4) is not indefensible according to the informal account of epistemic indefensibility quoted above. Let the persons a, b, c, be supposed to be abundantly endowed with logical acumen. Since we have stated clear conditions under which "$B_b B_c p$" is true under this assumption, how does the supposition of logical omniscience on the part of a require that he know our proposition to be false? It cannot.

Hintikka has acknowledged the correctness of these observations in his article "Knowledge, Belief, and Logical Consequences," where he says:

> The gist of the matter is that the intuitive account of "deductively perfect world" of "logically omniscient beings" . . . is seriously incomplete . . . ; *a satisfactory explanation of an "epistemically perfect world" must include the requirement that its inhabitants not only are deductively omniscient but that each of them knows and believes that they all are* . . . In one sense, the upshot of Linsky's and Wu's criticism is thus merely to point out the need of this revision of the intuitive (and semantical) explanation of the notions of self-sustenance, defensibility, etc. I do not see that this makes a major difference to the methodological situation as compared with *Knowledge and Belief.* [Hintikka, [KBLC], pp. 35–36; my italics]

He then continues,

> In particular, when the change just pointed out is made in the intuitive account of the notions of defensibility, self-sustenance, etc., all the different discrepancies between this account and the formal metalogical results which are discussed by Linsky and Wu disappear at once.

But this last statement is false, as can be shown, following Wu, by considering a slightly more complex case, similar to my earlier example. Consider the statement "$B_aB_bB_cp$" where, again, 'p' represents an inconsistent statement and $a, b,$ and c are different persons. This statement is formally indefensible by the same argument used above (with an additional application of (C.b*)). But what is the situation with regard to Hintikka's revised formulation of the informal concept of defensibility (the words italicized in Hintikka's remarks, quoted above)? Let us suppose that both "B_bB_cp" and "B_cp" are false. The person c is then not guilty of a failure of logical omniscience nor does he believe that anyone else is guilty of such a failure. Nor is the person b to be criticized on either ground, for, by supposition, "B_bB_cp" is false. Finally, the person a is not guilty of either charge, for let us suppose that he both realizes that p is inconsistent and believes that b and c are logically omniscient. How, then, can he believe that b believes that c believes p? He believes this because he does not believe that b believes that c is logically omniscient. What is required to rule out this case is an additional requirement for the person a. He must (1) realize that p is inconsistent, (2) believe that everyone is logically omniscient, and, further, he must (3) believe that everyone believes that everyone else is logically omniscient. Clearly, these conditions do not collapse, and they become more complex with each iteration of a modal operator without end. Hintikka's revision leaves Achilles always just one step behind the tortoise.

In her article, Wu described the situation quite accurately.

As a consequence, a statement cannot be embedded in a member μ of a model system Ω, if it could not be true under the ideal circumstance that everyone not only follows out all the logical consequences of what he knows and believes but also knows and believes that everyone follows out all the logical consequences of what he knows and believes and moreover knows and believes that everyone knows and believes that everyone follows out all the logical consequences of what he knows and believes and so on. [Wu, [HD], pp. 30–31]

In conclusion, Wu proposes the following as an adequate (implicitly recursive) account of the notion of defensibility that is formalized in Hintikka's epistemic and doxastic logic:

> A statement or set of statements is defensible if and only if it could be true under the ideal circumstance that everyone follows out all the logical consequences of what he knows and believes and everyone knows and believes that only defensible statements are true. [Ibid., p. 31]

Now these conditions are never realized; so what is the correct methodological position? One response might be put in the following way. The theorems of epistemic and doxastic logic are true only under highly idealized conditions that do not obtain, even approximately, in the real world. Therefore, it is not about actual knowledge and belief that we have anything to learn from the formal logic of these notions. An alternative response might be that it is actual garden-variety belief and knowledge whose logic is being investigated; only the knowers and believers are idealized. In either case the problem remains. What does the possible-worlds analysis of propositional attitudes have to teach us about our actual use of these concepts? The theorems that are the source of these difficulties are by-products of two central features of the logic of the propositional attitudes in its classical formulation. This logic is (1) a conservative extension of standard quantification theory (Hintikka's Theorem) and (2) is based on the possible-worlds analysis of modal concepts.

III

Propositional attitudes reject the substitutivity of identity. No other feature of the logic of the propositional attitudes has been so extensively studied and analyzed since Frege initiated the subject in his "On Sense and Reference" (1892). Quine has repeatedly urged the intimate connection between the substitutivity and the standard interpretation of quantification. This connection has been formulated as follows by Dagfinn Føllesdal:

> Any interpretation of quantifiers requires the traditional substitutivity axioms of identity, that is statements of the form: $(x)(y)$

$(x = y \supset . Fx \supset Fy)$ to be true (*Quine's thesis*). Here '*F*' stands for any predicate, simple or complex. [Føllesdal, [IQ], p. 271]

In his formulations of the logic of knowledge and belief, Hintikka has not adopted the unrestricted substitutivity of identity but, rather, a restricted form. It is obvious why he has restricted the substitutivity of identity to atomic formulas and identities. They are free of epistemic and doxastic operators, so the restriction blocks such sophisms as that given by Quine about Philip, Cicero, and Tully and similar arguments. But the restriction on substitutivity makes objectual quantification unintelligible when combined with propositional attitudes, as is maintained by Quine's thesis. To show this, I exhibit, following Føllesdal, a model set μ containing the following case of the denial of the substitutivity of identity:

(1)	$(\exists x)(\exists y)(x = y . K_b Fx . \sim K_b Fy)$	
(2)	$(\exists y)(a = y . K_b Fa . \sim K_b Fy)$	from (1) by (108)
(3)	$a = c . K_b Fa . \sim K_b Fc$	from (2) by (108)
(4)	Fa	3, Simp. (C.K)
(5)	Fc	4,3 (C.=)
(6)	$(\exists x) K_b (a = x)$	(2) (1), (108)
(7)	$(\exists x) K_b (c = x)$	(3) (2), (108)
(8)	$K_b (a = d)$	(6), (108)
(9)	$K_b (c = e)$	(7), (108)
(10)	$a = d$	(8), (C.K)
(11)	$c = e$	(9), (C.K)
(12)	Fd	(4), (10), (C.=)
(13)	Fe	(5), (11), (C.=)

Now consider a model system Ω, such that μ, $\mu^* \epsilon \Omega$ and μ^* is an epistemic alternative to μ (with respect to b) in Ω. μ^* contains:

(14)	$\sim Fc$	(3), (C.P*), (C.$\sim$K)
(15)	Fa	(3), (C.K*)
(16)	$a = d$	(8), (C.K)
(17)	$c = e$	(9), (C.K*)
(18)	$\sim Fe$	(14), (17), (C.=)
(19)	Fd	(15), (16), (C.=)

In the world (partially) described by the formulas in μ, which we may think of as the actual world, $a = c$. In this world a has the property F. Does a—i.e., c—have F in the world described by the formulas in μ^*? According to (15), it does, but, according to (14), it does not. So, contrary to our original supposition, μ^* does not describe a possible world at all.

These considerations only vindicate Quine's thesis that unrestricted substitutivity and the standard interpretation of quantifiers cannot be separated. $(\exists x)Fx$ says that there is something that has the property F, and $(\exists x)K_bFx$ is intended to mean that there is something such that b knows that it is F. On the possible-worlds account that we are considering, this means that there is something such that it has F in all epistemically possible worlds (with respect to b). Is $a(=c)$ such an object? It has F in the world described by the formulas in μ. In the world described by the formulas in μ^*, however, both Fa and $\sim Fc$ are true. Hence our question, whether $a(=c)$ has F in μ^*, cannot be given a coherent answer. It follows from this that the formula $(\exists x)K_b\,Fx$ is unintelligible. Quantifiers cannot intelligibly bind a variable within the scope of an epistemic operator. Quine's thesis is vindicated.

The only recourse in the face of this situation, if we are to retain the standard-quantifier rule of specification to constants, is to abandon the restricted-substitutivity principle (C.=) in favor of unrestricted substitutivity, that is, in favor of the principle that is like (C.=) except that the requirement that the formulas referred to in (C.=) must be either atomic or identities is removed. Hintikka calls this condition (C.=!). But will this not have the disastrous consequence of establishing the validity of Quine's sophism? Does it not have the further disastrous consequence that all true identities are known? Indeed, under the principle (C.=!) the following sentence is self-sustaining: $(x)\,(y)\,(x = y\,.\supset: K_a\,(x = y))$. This is established by *reductio ad absurdum* as follows:

(1)	"$(\exists x)(\exists y)[(x = y)\,\&$	
	$\sim K_a(x = y)]$"$\epsilon\mu$	counterassumption
(2)	"$(\exists y)[(b = y)\&\sim K_a(b = y)]$"$\epsilon\mu$	(1), (108)
(3)	"$(\exists x)K_a(x = b)$"$\epsilon\mu$	(1), (2), (108)
(4)	"$(b = c)\&\sim K_a(b = c)$"$\epsilon\mu$	(2), (108)

(5) "$(\exists x)K_a(x = c)$"$\epsilon\mu$	(2), (4), (108)
(6) "$P_a(b \neq c)$"$\epsilon\mu$	(4), (C.&), (C.~K)
(7) "$P_a(b \neq b)$"$\epsilon\mu$	(4), (6), (C.=!)
(8) "$b \neq b$"$\epsilon\mu*$	(7), (C.P*)

(8) contradicts (C.self=). Q.E.D.

Furthermore, the self-sustenance of the sentence

(9) $(a = b)\&K_cFa \supset K_cFb$

is an immediate consequence of the rule (C.=!). Apparently we are on the horns of a dilemma. The standard interpretation of quantifiers requires (C.=!), but this condition entails the validity of the formula (9) as well as the self-sustenance of the principle

(10) $(x)(y)[(x = y) \supset K_a(x = y)]$.

Alethic modalities face no such dilemma. The standard interpretation of quantifiers, we have seen, requires the unrestricted substitutivity of the terms of a true statement of identity. $(a = b)\&\Box Fa \supset \Box Fb$ is a theorem of alethic modal logic with the standard-quantifier rule of universal instantiation to constants; $a = b \supset \Box(a = b)$ is also a theorem. The latter principle entails, by semantic ascent, that the atomic singular terms (proper names) of alethic modal logic are rigid designators, and this removes the air of paradox about these principles. If Hesperus is Phosphorus in the actual world, there cannot be a possible world in which Hesperus $\neq$ Phosphorus, for that would be a world in which Hesperus $\neq$ Hesperus—not a possible world. Similarly, whatever property belongs to Hesperus in any possible world belongs also to Phosphorus in that world. To deny this is to suppose that, in a possible world W, there is some property F that belongs to Hesperus that does not belong to Phosphorus (=Hesperus), and this is incoherent. $a = b \supset K_d(a = b)$, and $(a = b)\&K_dFa \supset K_dFb$, and their doxastic analogues, are self-sustaining sentences of the logic of knowledge and belief, given the unrestricted substitutivity of identity required for the standard interpretation of quantifiers. As in the alethic case, these principles require the atomic singular terms (proper names) that

93

occur in the sentences of epistemic and doxastic logic to be epistemically (doxastically) rigid designators. But now this result creates paradoxes that, in the alethic case, it removed. After all, ordinary proper names *are* alethically rigid designators. When I say that Nixon might have lost the 1968 presidential election or told the truth about Watergate, it is Nixon I am referring to—the same man in all of the alternative alethically possible worlds. But it would be absurd to maintain that 'Hesperus' and 'Phosphorus' are doxastically rigid designators (designate the same object in all doxastically possible worlds), for then no one could ever believe that Hesperus is not Phosphorus or believe that Cicero denounced Catiline and not believe that Tully also denounced Catiline. This last statement is proved by the following argument:

(1) "Hesperus = Phosphorus"$\epsilon\mu$ assumption
(2) "B_a (Hesperus $\neq$ Phosphorus)"$\epsilon\mu$ assumption
(3) "Hesperus $\neq$ Phosphorus"$\epsilon\mu^*$ 2, (C.b*)

Statement (1) entails, by semantic ascent, that 'Hesperus' and 'Phosphorus' denote the same thing in the world described by the sentences in μ. Statement (3) entails, by semantic ascent, that 'Hesperus' and 'Phosphorus' denote different objects in the possible world described by the sentences in μ^*. Hence, these names do not denote the same thing in all doxastically possible worlds; that is, they are not doxastically rigid designators. How are we to make this situation intelligible to ourselves? Hesperus (= Phosphorus) is (are?) *two* objects in the world described by the sentences in μ^*. It is not just that 'Hesperus' and 'Phosphorus' are names of different objects, for that is easily enough understood. The problem is that in this world Hesperus (= Phosphorus) is not Phosphorus (= Hesperus). That cannot be understood at all.

IV

We have shown some difficulties encountered by the possible-worlds analysis of propositional attitudes that are not forthcoming for this account of alethic modality. In conclusion, I would like to indicate a respect in which the two types of possible-worlds accounts are actually incompatible with each other. Consider the statement 'George IV believes that Hesperus $\neq$ Phosphorus'. On the present account, this says that, in at least one possible world compatible with what George IV believes, Hesperus $\neq$ Phosphorus. But 'Hesperus' and 'Phosphorus' are alethically rigid designators; hence there is no alethically possible world in which it is the case that Hesperus $\neq$ Phosphorus. The possible worlds involved in a person's beliefs are doxastically possible alternatives to his actual belief-states; that is, they are mutually compatible sets of beliefs that are each compatible with the person's actual beliefs. But how can a world be "possible" in any sense—alethically, epistemically, or doxastically—if some of the statements true in it are alethically impossible? The present account requires that some of these doxastically possible worlds be alethically impossible, at least if George IV is to believe that Hesperus $\neq$ Phosphorus.

A problem very like this one was considered in section II, above. The principles of epistemic (doxastic) logic are applicable only to idealized knowers (believers), who know (believe) all of the logical consequences of what they know (believe). In particular, then, they know and believe all logical truths. It is clear why such idealization is required by the possible-worlds analysis of the propositional attitudes. People cannot believe logical falsehoods because there are no possible worlds (compatible with everything they believe) in which logical falsehoods are true. One then defends this analysis of the attitudes by claiming that, though the knowers and believers are idealized (logically omniscient) with respect to the content of their propositional attitudes, still, the attitudes analyzed are garden-variety knowledge and belief. Now one more dose of the same medicine can cure the difficulty arising from the necessary truth of 'Hesperus $=$ Phosphorus'. What is required is further idealization: our knowers and believers must be not only logically omniscient but also metaphysically omniscient. They must know and believe all necessary truths. Of course, while this saves the possible-worlds account of the propositional attitudes, it leaves us with our problem about George IV. How are we to analyze his belief that Hesperus $\neq$ Phosphorus or his belief that Scott's parents are other than his actual parents, assuming that it is a necessary truth that Scott has the parents he has? George IV can believe these things, on the account under consideration, only if some of the doxastically possible worlds that must be considered in accounting for his beliefs are (alethically) impossible. That is the only possible alternative, and Hintikka accepts it in a later publication (Hintikka, [IPWV]).

V

How is Hintikka's doxastic logic related to the intensional logics of Frege and Russell? In a sense they are not rivals, for they operate at different levels. The intensional logics of Frege and Russell provide an account of the logical form of intensional contexts, including an account of the values of the variables appearing in the logistic formulation of these contexts. Neither Frege nor Russell provides a *theory* of intensional concepts like knowledge, belief, and assertion if providing a theory is understood to involve giving axioms characterizing these concepts and distinguishing them from each other. Such a theory would aim to decide such issues as this: *If a person knows (believes) that p, does that person know (believe) that he knows (believes) that p?* Hintikka, on the other hand, does provide an axiomatic characterization of knowledge and belief that aims to decide just such questions, but he does not first carry through the task of characterizing the logical form of statements involving these concepts. In *Knowledge and Belief,* quantifiers are used only together with individual variables. Formulas such as $B_a p$ and $K_a p$ appear, and the role of the letter 'p' is explained to be that of holding a place for a declarative sentence. Quantifiers are never used together with such letters, and no interpretation is given for such constructions. We cannot, then, within these systems, formulate even such a belief as that held by Peter Ramus, that everything Aristotle said was false.

Hintikka is simply silent about what, if anything, are to be the values of his sentential letters. He does not really treat them as objectual variables at all. But the logic he develops is very close to that which follows from adopting logical equivalence as the criterion of propositional identity in logical systems that do genuinely quantify over propositions. While Russell and Frege provide no explicit conditions for propositional identity, it is clear from their discussions that they reject logical equivalence. Under this criterion, all distinction between logical truths is obliterated, and similarly for logical falsehoods. There is just one logical truth and one falsehood. Logical truths are true in all possible worlds, and logical falsehoods in none, if it is a necessary condition, for a world to be possible, that it be logically possible. Hence the requirement of logical omniscience. Any theory provides an idealized model rather than a naturalistic description of the phenomenon it explains. I have stated that Hintikka's theory, nevertheless, carries idealization in a direction that is unsuitable for giving an account of logical features that are *distinctive* of the propositional attitudes, for it assimilates them to logical necessity. The entire argument can just as well be viewed as an examination of the consequences of taking logical equivalence as the condition of propositional identity. It is this that forces the requirement of logical omniscience.

A List of Hintikka's Conditions on Model Sets
Cited in Proofs in This Chapter

(C.b*) If "$B_a p$"$\epsilon\mu$ and if μ belongs to a model system Ω, then there is in Ω at least one doxastic alternative μ^* to μ (with respect to a) such that $p\epsilon\mu^*$.

(C.K) If "$K_a p$"$\epsilon\mu$, then $p\epsilon\mu$.

(C.K*) If "$K_a p$"$\epsilon\mu$ and if μ^* is an epistemic alternative to μ (with respect to a) in some model system, then $p\epsilon\mu^*$.

(C.P*) If "$P_a p$"$\epsilon\mu$ and if μ belongs to a model system Ω, then there is in Ω at least one epistemic alternative μ^* to μ (with respect to a) such that $p\epsilon\mu^*$.

(C.~K) If "$\sim K_a p$"$\epsilon\mu$, then "$P_a \sim p$"$\epsilon\mu$.

(C.~~) If "$\sim\sim p$"$\epsilon\mu$, then $p\epsilon\mu$.

(C.&) If "$p \& q$" $\epsilon\mu$, then $p\epsilon\mu$ and $q\epsilon\mu$.

(C.=) If $p\epsilon\mu$, "$a = b$"$\epsilon\mu$, and if p is an atomic formula or an identity, and if q is like p, except that a and b have been interchanged in one or several places, then $q\epsilon\mu$.

(C.=!) Like (C.=), except that it is not limited to atomic formulas and identities.

(C.self=) If a occurs in the formulas of μ, "$a = a$"$\epsilon\mu$.

(108) If "$(\exists x)p$"$\epsilon\mu$, then for at least one free individual symbol a we have $p(a/x)\epsilon\mu$ and "$(\exists x)K_b(a = x)$"$\epsilon\mu$, provided that there are in p no epistemic operators different from "K_b" and "P_b" and that x occurs within the scope of one of them in p.

6

Quine on Quantifying In

Lo que Quine ha logrado mostrar, al parecer, es que sus preferencias estrictamente extensionalistas tienen el efecto de excluir por completo la lógica modal.

Alonzo Church

The study of quantified modal logic was initiated nearly simultaneously by Ruth Barcan Marcus and Rudolf Carnap in the mid-1940s with papers published in the *Journal of Symbolic Logic*—Marcus with "A Functional Calculus of First Order Based on Strict Implication" (see Barcan, [FCFOSI]), Carnap with "Modalities and Quantification" (Carnap, [MQ]). From the very inception of the subject, Quine became its critic, developing an attack against it that has continued and deepened over the following decades down to the present. The attack focuses on one feature of quantified modality: the binding of a variable within a modal context by a quantifier lying outside the scope of the modality. The problem raised by Quine's critique, the problem of "quantifying in," is the central issue in the dispute over the legitimacy of any language in which quantifiers mix freely with modal operators. The critique applies across the whole range of modalities, from strictly logical (alethic) modalities, such as the modalities of necessity and possibility, to propositional attitudes, such as belief. In this chapter I critically review these criticisms insofar as they turn on the particular logical feature of nonextensional contexts that has played so central a role in the present study: the failure of substitutivity of coreferential singular terms. I present Russellian and Fregean responses to Quine's criticisms. The discussion is carried on, for the most part, with examples of logical necessity as the relevant modality, but it should be emphasized that all these considerations apply, with but minor modifications, to belief and other propositional attitudes as well.

I

Singular terms and the sign of identity are intimately connected in the semantics and syntax of classical logic, which requires this sign to be flanked by these terms in well-formed sentences. The intimate connection is emphasized by Quine in "Reference and Modality," where he explicates its logical significance in his *principle of substitutivity:* "The terms of a true statement of identity are everywhere intersubstitutive, *salva veritate*" (Quine, [R&M], p. 139). Given the truth of 'Socrates is the teacher of Plato' and 'The teacher of Plato is the husband of Xanthippe', the principle yields the truth of 'Socrates is the husband of Xanthippe'. This is different from the principle formulated in definition *13.01 of *Principia Mathematica,* which identifies identity with indiscernibility as follows:

(1) $(x = y) = (\phi) (\phi!x \supset \phi!y)$ Df.

Wittgenstein, in the *Tractatus,* objects to this identification. The objection is that "Russell's definition of '=' is inadequate, because according to it we cannot say that two objects have all their properties in common. (Even if this proposition is never correct, it still has sense)" (*Tractatus,* 5.5302). (1) says not only that, if x and y are identical, they share all their properties; it provides for the converse as well: that objects cannot, in Leibniz's phrase, differ *solo numero*. Wittgenstein's objection is to *this* implication of Russell's definition. The idea of objects differing only numerically has been introduced solely that it may be set aside. It is not at issue in the *principle of the indiscernibility of identicals,* which states that identical objects have the same properties (do not differ qualitatively). One may or may not agree with Wittgenstein that qualitative identity does not entail numerical identity, but one cannot coherently think that numerical identity does not entail the qualitative sort.

The principle of substitutivity appears to be merely a formal-mode version of the indiscernibility of identicals; but though it lacks the self-evidence of the latter, its justification is easily found in classical semantic considerations. Logic teaches us to analyze statements as arising from open sentences by binding their free variables or by replacing these by singular terms. Open sentences are expressions that are true of certain objects and false of others. For example, a true statement results from the open sentence 'x is a Greek' when some name, or other singular designation, for some object of which the open sentence is true replaces the variable 'x'. Given this semantical analysis, together with some further details, we see why the principle of substitutivity has been accepted; for that the terms of a true identity-statement are everywhere intersubstitutive, *salva veritate,* is merely explicative of the idea of singular terms having singular reference. The reasoning is as follows. By replacing, with an appropriate variable, any singular term in one or more of its occurrences in each statement containing at least one singular term, we construct a class of (one-place) open sentences. Any singular term thus replaced in a true statement refers to an object that satisfies the open sentence thus constructed. An object satisfies such an open sentence only if replacing the open sentence's free variable by *any* singular term making reference to the object turns the open sentence into a true statement. (The converse of this conditional is not correct, because it is not assumed that every object in the range of our variables is designated by some singular term. The conditional itself holds for all objects in the range of our variables, albeit vacuously of those without designations.) Consequently, the result of replacing a singular term in a true statement by any other singular term referring to the same object leaves the truth-value of the host statement unchanged. Terms of a true identity-statement refer to the same thing. And with this we have a proof of the principle of substitutivity.

II

The principle of substitutivity is explicative not only of the concept of singular reference but of the concept of quantification as well. $(\exists x)F(x)$ is true if, and only if, there is at least one object in the range of the variable that satisfies the open sentence $F(x)$. If it be granted that $F(a)$ is true (where 'a' is a singular term) and that it remains true under substitution of coreferential terms for 'a', then, by the semantical account already given, we have our satisfying object in a.

Consequently, $(\exists x)F(x)$ is also true. The inference by existential generalization is justified, because in performing it we are merely abstracting from the particular mode of designating an object in a true statement where no particular mode of designation is relevant to the truth of that statement. Failure of the inference from $F(a)$ to $(\exists x)F(x)$ occurs if, and only if, 'a' fails of singular reference in $F(a)$. For example, the inference from 'Pegasus does not exist' to '$(\exists x)(x$ does not exist)' fails because nothing satisfies the open sentence 'x does not exist'. Failure of substitutivity for a term in a given context entails failure of reference for that term in that context. For this reason, by the present argument, it entails failure of existential generalization on that term as well. Contexts productive of failure of substitutivity are for this reason called by Quine "referentially opaque." Quine takes his argument to show that we cannot sensibly quantify into referentially opaque contexts.

III

The principle of substitutivity has now come to be seen as an integral part of the semantics of classical quantification theory. On the other hand, as already noted, hardly is the principle stated before one finds cases apparently contrary to it. The true identity 'Cicero = Tully' will not support the substitution of 'Cicero' for 'Tully' in ' 'Tully' consists of five letters'. This is not a genuine paradox, for *substitutivity* is wrongly applied to terms in contexts in which they do not refer "simply" to their designations. ' 'Tully' consists of five letters' is not about Cicero (= Tully) but about one of his names. According to Quine, lapse of substitutivity merely reveals that the occurrence of the name supplanted is not "purely referential" because "the statement depends not only on the object but on the form of the name" (Quine, [R&M], p. 140). Quotation is only the most blatant of contexts in which terms can fail of purely referential occurrence. Consider 'Philip believes that Tegucigalpa is in Nicaragua'. Misuse of *substitutivity* will take us from this and 'Tegucigalpa = the capital of Honduras' to the falsehood 'Philip believes that the capital of Honduras is in Nicaragua'. Here again, for Quine, failure of substitutivity is only symptomatic of 'Tegucigalpa's failure of purely referential occurrence at the place of substitution. As he says, ". . . the contexts 'is unaware that . . .' and 'believes that . . .' *resemble* the context of single quotes in this respect: a name may occur referentially in a statement S and yet not occur referentially in a longer statement which is formed by embedding S in the context 'is unaware that . . .' or 'believes that . . .' " [Quine, ibid., p. 142]. For Quine these contexts are all referentially opaque, and logical necessity provides but another example. It is a true contingent statement that

(2)   9 = the number of the planets.

It is further true that

(3) $\Box (9 > 7)$.

But replacement of '9' in (3) by 'the number of the planets' in virtue of (2) yields

(4) $\Box$ (the number of the planets > 7),

which is false.

Quine's concepts of the referentially opaque context and the purely referential occurrence of singular terms reflect the standpoint of the semantics of classical extensional predicate logic. From that standpoint, the principle of substitutivity is analytic of the idea of singular reference, and we are left with no alternative but to conclude that '9' in $\Box(9 > 7)$ does not make singular reference to 9. We cannot, in our semantics, make the view coherent that '9' refers to the object 9 in (3), in view of the truth of (2) and (3) and the falsity of (4). Quine's terminology leaves us to suppose that terms that fail to refer "simply" to their objects (or that fail of "purely" referential occurrence) might, in some unexplained fashion, still manage to refer but do so only nonpurely or nonsimply. But this part of his theory is never developed, and I believe that his view is really that, in non-extensional contexts, singular terms do not refer at all.

Referential opacity poses a problem because our semantics is inapplicable to opaque contexts. $\Box(9 > 7)$ does not, on analysis, yield an open sentence $\Box(x > 7)$ from which it results by replacement of 'x' by '9'. $\Box(x > 7)$ cannot, coherently, be taken as an open sentence; for given an open sentence and an object within the range of its variable, either the open sentence is true or it is false of that object. Is our purported open sentence true of the object 9? Since the number of planets *is* 9, an affirmative answer is incompatible with the falsity of (4), and a negative answer is incompatible with the truth of (3). Thus, $\Box(x > 7)$ is not an open sentence at all. But if the numeral '9' does not name an object in $\Box(9 > 7)$ that satisfies the open sentence $\Box(x > 7)$, what role is it performing there? How is its presence relevant to the truth of the sentence containing it? Our inability to answer this question reveals that we do not know the logical form of such statements.

We explored above the intimate connection in classical semantics between singular terms and quantification. The inference by existential generalization from $F(a)$ to $(\exists x)F(x)$ is valid if and only if 'a' makes singular reference in $F(a)$. We had to abandon the view that, in (3), '9' refers to 9. It is an easy step to conclude, and Quine does conclude, that

(5) $(\exists x)\Box(x > 7)$

is unintelligible; we cannot sensibly *quantify into* referentially opaque contexts. What (5) *seems* to say is that there is something such that it is necessarily greater than 7. But Quine asks, "What is this number which, according to (5), is necessarily greater than 7? According to (3), from which (5) was inferred, it was 9, that is, the number of planets; but to suppose this would conflict with the fact that (4) is false" (Quine, [R&M], p. 148; I have altered the original numbering of Quine's formulas). The difficulty arises because necessary or contingent traits of objects are taken to belong to them not absolutely but according to whether one way of specifying them is used rather than another. Nine is taken to have necessary greaterness than seven according as it is specified in (3) but not as in (4). Hence the difference in truth-value between (3) and (4) and the consequent obscurity of (5). The modal logician, saddled as he is with (5), is thus committed to a metaphysical view ("Aristotelian essentialism," to give it a name) according to which necessary and contingent properties do belong to objects irrespective of their modes of specification, if they are specified at all. It is a doctrine that is required to make sense of

103

(5) in spite of the difference in truth-value of (3) and (4) and the truth of (2), i.e., in spite of the classical extensional semantics of quantification. "Evidently," says Quine, "this reversion to Aristotelian essentialism is required if quantification into modal contexts is to be insisted on." He concludes: "So much the worse for quantified modal logic" (Quine, [R&M], pp. 155–56). Quine's arguments in this section apply as well to belief and other propositional attitudes as they do to necessity.

IV

We have assumed that, if '9' names an object in (3), what it names is 9. By abandoning the assumption that in opaque contexts names stand for their ordinary references, Frege is able to provide an analysis that does not take these contexts as productive of reference failure. (Frege rejected the idea of modal logic. What is presented here is an extension of his views.) From a Fregean point of view, such contexts are incorrectly characterized as "referentially opaque." For Frege, they are, according to the method of indirect discourse (see chap. 3, above) producers of reference shift rather than reference failure, and he calls them "oblique." The references of names in oblique contexts are, according to this method, what are, in ordinary contexts, their senses. For Frege it is false that '9' in (2) and '9' in (3) have the same reference; there is a fallacy of ambiguity, as we have seen, in passing from (2) and (3) to (4). So, for him, there is no such thing as referential opacity where the criterion for this is failure of substitutivity. In (2), '9' has the same reference as 'the number of the planets' but a different sense. This sense is the (oblique) reference of '9' in (3).

Quine, in an early paper, "Notes on Existence and Necessity" (Quine, [NEN], pp. 83–84), exploits a distinction between *meaning* and *designation* that is like Frege's distinction between sense and reference. If we pursue the similarity and adopt, for Quine's pair of concepts, the principle that in oblique contexts the designations of names are their meanings, we have a proof at hand that there are no opaque contexts. On our Fregean assumption, the principle of substitutivity allows replacement of names in oblique contexts only by synonymous names; and reference now is taken as context-relative.

Hence the principle of substitutivity is recast so as to affirm the replaceability of any term in a given context by any other term having the same reference as the first *in that context*. Since we cannot change the meaning of a statement, ordinary or oblique, by replacing any of its constituents by a synonym, such substitution cannot change truth-values. If, with Quine, we take failure of substitutivity as a criterion of referential opacity (Quine, [R&M], p. 140, n.), there are no longer any referentially opaque contexts. By shifting the domain of discourse, we retain our semantics, and the old analysis continues its applicability to the misnamed opaque contexts.

V

If we assume, with Frege, that the reference of a complex name is a function of the references of its constituent names and that the reference of a (declarative) sentence is its truth-value, we have a proof that $\Box(9 > 7)$ remains true under every replacement of '9' by a name having the same ordinary sense as '9', provided that '9' is assumed to name that sense in that sentence. Under this last assumption, $\Box(x > 7)$ may be treated as an open sentence true of this sense. Failure of substitutivity in oblique contexts reveals that the relevant names differ in their ordinary senses. In *Die Grundlagen der Arithmetik,* to defend his thesis that numbers are objects, Frege thought it necessary to provide a sense for statements of identity between numbers, and between numbers and other objects (Frege, [FA], p. 73). If, now, we take senses to be objects, we must also provide them with identity-conditions. It is somewhat surprising that Frege himself made no attempt to do this in his published work. In Quine's phrase, "No entity without identity" (cited by Charles Parsons, [FTN], p. 18).

But, far from paving the way for the happy marriage of quantification and modality, Frege's theory of reference, Quine suggests, makes the union inevitably barren. On Frege's view, what can we make of statements in which names appear both inside and outside the scope of opacity-inducing operators? Consider

(6)   9 is greater than 7, and necessarily 9 is greater than 7.

According to Frege, the object here said to be greater than 7 is not the same as the object said to be necessarily greater than 7. But this is not what is intended in (6). (6) is intended as synonymous with

(7)   9 is greater than 7, and necessarily it is greater than 7.

The difficulty is that, for Frege, (7) should be sheer nonsense because the pronoun 'it' inside the scope of the modal operator cannot pick up the reference of the numeral '9' outside the scope of that operator. If the pronoun did pick up the reference of that numeral, it would refer to the object 9 rather than a sense, and this Frege denies. Since pronouns are the equivalents of the bound variables of natural language, we see, Quine says, that Frege's theory is incapable of reflecting the interplay between occurrences of terms both inside and outside the scope of modal operators that statements of modality are usually taken to express. We have an argument against the intelligibility of quantification into oblique contexts.

In the preceding paragraph, Quine's argument is made in accordance with what I have called, above, "the method of indirect discourse." This consists of an application, on my part, of what he actually says, for Quine directs his argument, in the first place, against Church's version of Frege's theory, and Church employs the method of direct discourse.

> Instead of a necessity operator attachable to sentences, he [Church] has a necessity predicate attachable to complex names of certain intensional objects called propositions. What makes this departure more serious than it sounds is that the constants and variables occurring in a sentence do not recur in Church's name of the corresponding proposition. Thus the interplay, usual in modal logic, between occurrences of expressions outside modal contexts and recurrences of them inside modal contexts, is ill reflected in Church's system. [Quine, [R&M], pp. 153–54]

My discussion in the two preceding paragraphs follows Quine's argument from the second (revised) edition of his *From a Logical Point of View* (1961) (Quine, [FLPV]). In a still later revision, which appeared in 1980, the argument is greatly altered. In fact, Quine admits, in the Preface to the new edition, that it is mistaken. It is not the case that the interplay between occurrences of expressions inside the scope of a modal operator and outside that scope cannot be relfected in the Frege-Church account. Quine had missed the significance of Church's primitive function Δ, which maps intensional objects onto their extensions as values. The interplay between expressions inside and outside the scope of modal operators is then mediated through this function. The connections are not severed; they are only mediated.

When Frege came to deal with oblique contexts, he decided that names in them referred to their ordinary senses and not to their ordinary references. Suppose that identity-statements that are not merely true but necessarily true must contain terms whose ordinary senses are the same. This condition for identity of sense for contexts of alethic modality is hardly avoidable. Then, given Frege's principle identifying oblique reference with ordinary sense in the method of indirect discourse, necessary identity-statements would sustain substitution in necessity contexts. If we now further suppose that all true identity-statements are necessarily true, all our purported examples of the referential opacity of necessity will be swept aside and safely accounted for as fallacies of ambiguity.

At one time Quine thought that by intensionalizing the values of our variables in this way we would render all true identities necessarily true and so clear the way to quantified modal logic. In a letter to Rudolf Carnap, published in Carnap's *Meaning and Necessity,* Quine says,

> I agree that such adherence to an intensional ontology, with extrusion of extensional entities altogether from the range of values of the variables, is indeed an effective way of reconciling quantification and modality. The cases of conflict between quantification and modality depend on extensions as values of variables. In your object language we may unhesitatingly quantify modalities because extensions have been dropped from among the values of the variables; even the individuals of the concrete world have disappeared, leaving only their concepts behind them. [Carnap, [*MN*], p. 197]

The purging of concrete individuals from the universe of discourse, Quine thought, would leave us with intensional objects no one of which could be uniquely specified by alternative conditions that fail of logical equivalence.

I am unable to construct an even apparently plausible argument that the purification suggested by Quine would have such beneficial consequences. At any rate, he was wrong about this and he says so. (However, he never seems to have recognized that it was not Church's idea.) "As a matter of fact, the worrisome charge that quantified modal logic can tolerate only intensions and not classes or individuals was a mistake to begin with. . . . Now on this latter point Church was wrong. I have been slow to see it, but the proof is simple" (Quine, [*WP*], pp. 183–84). Suppose the condition 'ψx' uniquely to determine the object x. Then, where 'p' is any truth not implied by 'ψx', '$p . \psi x$' also uniquely determines x. But the two conditions 'ψx' and '$p . \psi x$' are contingently, not logically, coincident. This argument does not depend on the extensionality of x, so intensionalizing the values of the variables will not avoid it.

Suppose that we go at it the other way around and simply exclude those objects from our domain of discourse that admit of unique specifications by conditions that fail of necessary equivalence. If we do this, ". . . there ceases to be any such objection to quantifying into modal position. Thus we can legitimize quantification into modal position by postulating that whenever each of two open sentences uniquely determines one and the same object x, the sentences are equivalent by necessity" (Quine, [*WO*], p. 197). We can put this opacity-annihilating postulate thus, where 'Fx' and 'Gx' are arbitrary open sentences and 'Fx and x only' is short for '$(w)(Fw$ if and only if $w = x)$':

(8) If Fx and x only and Gx and x only then (necessarily $(w)(Fw$ if and only if Gw)).

But this postulate annihilates modal distinctions along with the referential opacity of necessity. For letting 'p' stand for any true sentence, it can be shown that necessarily p. Let y be any object and let $x = y$. Then

(9) (p and $x = y$) and x only

and

(10) $x = y$ and x only.

Next, in our postulate take 'Fx' as '$p \cdot x = y$' and 'Gx' as '$x = y$'. It follows from (9) and (10) that

(11)   Necessarily $(w)((p$ and $w = y)$ if and only if $w = y)$.

(11) implies '$(p$ and $y = y)$ if and only if $y = y$', which implies p. Hence, since what is implied by a necessary truth is a necessary truth, (11) implies that necessarily p. Q.E.D. Modal distinctions collapse (Quine, [*WO*], p. 198).

Here the argument against intensions as values for the variables of quantified modal logic is carried through without deployment of singular terms. But it can be carried through by making use of them as well, according to Quine. The rationale behind the recourse to intensions as values for the variables of quantified modal logic was, according to him, in the first place, the consideration that intensions seemed to have the right sort of names for their job. Names for intensions were supposed to satisfy the condition that any two of them naming the same intension would be terms of a necessarily true statement of identity. A modal logic that confined its domain of discourse to intensions would thus be free of referentially opaque contexts.

Intensions, with the obscurity of their identity-conditions, may be, as Quine says, "creatures of darkness." But if the above-stated condition on their names is taken as analytic of them, it can be shown, as Quine subsequently realized, that they do not exist at all. The argument is Quine's own:

For, where A is any intensional object, say an attribute, and 'p' stands for an arbitrarily true sentence, clearly,

(35) $A = (\imath x)[p \cdot (x = A)]$.

Yet, if the true statement represented by 'p' is not analytic, then neither is (35), and its sides are no more interchangeable in

> modal contexts than are 'Evening Star' and 'Morning Star', or
> '9' and 'the number of planets'. [Quine, [R&M], p. 153]

What is refuted here is not Church's actual view but Quine's mistaken interpretation of it, which he attributes to Church in his second paragraph following this quotation.

What emerges from these considerations—from this survey of Quine's arguments against the intensional approach to modality and his subsequent retractions—is that Quine failed from the start to appreciate the rationale behind the intensional point of view. He saw, of course, that the central feature of the intensional approach adopted by Frege, Carnap, and Church is that intensions are more finely discriminated than extensions. Expressions can agree in extension and differ in intension. Now, failure of substitutivity in modal contexts can be explained as arising because, in modal contexts, names denote these more finely individuated intensions. Modal paradoxes, such as Quine's about nine and the number of the planets, arise from taking the relevant terms as denoting the more crudely discriminated extensions. Quine's mistaken assumption was that intensions could serve their purpose only by being the kind of object that is specifiable only by conditions having the feature that, if they specified the same such object, they could not fail of necessary equivalence. Correspondingly, he mistakenly assumed that intensions are objects such that any two singular terms having the same one as denotation do so necessarily; i.e., their having the same object as denotation could never be merely a contingent fact. Of course, if these assumptions were true, they would eliminate all cases of failure of substitutivity in modal contexts under the intensional interpretation. But they are not true, as Quine's own subsequent counterexamples show. No entities, extensional or intensional, satisfy these assumptions as long as the language contains any contingent truths at all. Quine's medicine is too strong. It kills the patient. What is required for eliminating the failures of substitutivity in modal and propositional attitude contexts, which disturb Quine and which are the source of the problem of "quantifying in," is, from a Fregean viewpoint, only more careful attention to the reference shift entailed by modal and propositional attitude constructions. These constructions can then be seen to be completely comfortable with the existence of conditions that uniquely determine an object and yet fail of logical equivalence.

What then, in the end, still stands as legitimate in Quine's critique of the intensional approach? The charge of obscurity, caused by the absence of clear principles of individuation for intensions, is a legitimate one and must be met by advocates of the intensional point of view. Quine's claim that to combine quantification and modality entails essentialism is a complex one, but on some legitimate interpretations it can be seen to be importantly right.

VII

Objections to Quine's arguments can be made on Russellian grounds as well. In presenting his paradoxes, such as the one about nine and the number of the planets, Quine regularly ignores the distinction, crucial for Russell's treatment of such paradoxes, between proper names and definite descriptions. He prefers to carry on his discussion in terms of an undifferentiated category of "singular terms." One might argue that all of Quine's difficulties in interpreting modal logic, insofar as they turn on the anomalous behavior of singular terms, together with the recourse to intensions, can be avoided by scrupulous attention to Russell's distinction between proper names and definite descriptions, together with the scope distinctions attendant upon the latter. We turn now to consideration of the Russellian view.

The view was elaborated by A. F. Smullyan in his paper "Modality and Description" (Smullyan, [MD], pp. 31–37). According to Smullyan, sentence (3) of Quine's argument in section III above is unambiguous—it is analyzed simply as $\Box(F(y))$; and the identity-premiss (2) has the form $y = (\imath x)(\phi x)$. But the conclusion (4) of Quine's argument is ambiguous, for it can be understood to accord the description large scope, i.e., to be of the form

$$(12) \quad [(\imath x)(\phi x)] \Box F(\imath x)(\phi x),$$

or (4) can be understood to accord the description narrow scope, i.e., as being of the form

$$(13) \quad \Box[(\imath x)(\phi x)] F(\imath x)(\phi x).$$

The distinction is the same as that between an assertion of the form

> (14) The so-and-so satisfies the condition that it is neces-
> sary that $F(x)$

and an assertion of the form

> (15) It is necessary that the so-and-so satisfies the condi-
> tion that $F(x)$.

Here is Smullyan's illustration of the difference.

> I will ask the reader to believe that James is now thinking of the
> number 3. If, now, someone were to remark 'There is one and
> only one integer which James is now thinking of and that
> integer is necessarily odd,' then he would be stating a con-
> tingent truth. For that there is just one integer which James now
> thinks of, is only an empirical fact. This statement could just
> as well be expressed in the form [14], 'The integer, which
> James is now thinking of, satisfies the condition that it is
> necessarily odd.' In contrast, the statement, 'It is necessary that
> James's integer is odd,' which is of the form [15], is an impos-
> sible statement and not a contingent one. If not necessary then
> necessarily not necessary: at least, so we assume. [Smullyan,
> [MD], p. 31]

Quine's mistake, according to Smullyan, following Russell, is to
ignore the ambiguity of (4) in Quine's example (see section III
above). Quine assumes it to be of the form (13), for he assumes that
(4) is false. But understood as exemplifying the form (13), (4) does
not follow from the premises. Understood as being of the form (12),
(4) does follow by substitutivity; but there is no paradox here, for,
thus understood, (4) is true. But is this last contention as clearly true
as Smullyan thinks it to be? When the description is eliminated, (12)
becomes

> (16) $(\exists c)(x)\{(\phi x) \equiv (x = c).\Box(Fc)\}$.

Smullyan apparently sees no problem in making sense of such constructions. Has Quine not shown that the attempt to bind a variable

in a referentially opaque context by a quantifier outside the context produces nonsense? According to Quine, (16) is nonsense, so it cannot represent a possible sense of (4). Thus Smullyan's argument from ambiguity is destroyed. Adherents of Smullyan's and Russell's viewpoint will answer that Quine's *argument* for the unintelligibility of constructions such as (16) rests on the fallacy of ambiguity exposed by them. Quine's response to Smullyan and Russell assumes the unintelligibility of such constructions as (16); he does not really prove this. Smullyan's argument against Quine assumes the intelligibility of these quantifications, but no attempt is made to explain them. Thus both Quine and Smullyan can each find the other begging the question at issue. "Notice to begin with" says Quine,

> that if we are to bring out Russell's distinction of scopes we must make two contrasting applications of Russell's contextual definition of description. But when the description is in a non-substitutive position, one of the two contrasting applications of the contextual definition is going to require quantifying into a non-substitutive position. So the appeal to scopes of descriptions does not justify such quantification, it just begs the question. [Quine, in Davidson and Hintikka, [*W&O*], p. 338]

Quine's second reason for rejecting the recourse to the theory of descriptions in defense of modality rests on his theory of the "primacy of predicates." According to Quine, all constant singular terms are eliminable in favor of general terms and bound variables. So if referential opacity is worth worrying about, it must show its symptoms when the constant singular terms are gone. The argument against quantifying into opaque contexts can then, however, still be made. Take the sentence

(17) $(\exists x)$(necessarily x is odd).

> . . . let us ban singular terms other than variables. We can still specify things; instead of specifying them by designation we specify them by conditions that uniquely determine them. On this approach we can still challenge the coherence of [17], by asking that such an object x be specified. One answer is that

[18] $(\exists y)(y \neq x = yy = y + y + y)$.

113

But the same number x is uniquely determined also by this different condition: there are x planets. Yet [18] entails 'x is odd' and thus evidently sustains 'necessarily x is odd', while 'there are x planets' does not. [Quine, ibid., p. 339]

Sentence (18) and 'there are x planets' uniquely specify the same object. Does that object verify (17)? We might answer "yes" if we start from (18) since it entails 'x is odd'. But, if we start from 'there are x planets', we will answer "no," since this latter specification does not entail 'x is odd'. Thus we are unable to specify an object that verifies (17). The idea of there being an object that is necessarily odd is incoherent. The only recourse for the modal logician is to a doctrine of essentialism according to which (18) is germane to (17), since it specifies its object essentially, while 'there are x planets' specifies that same object accidentally and thus is irrelevant to (17).

Quine's view is that we can make sense of modal statements only so long as we interpret them relative to particular modes of designating the objects referred to in them. Thus (3) is true of the object 9 relative to its specification by '9', but (4), though it attributes the same property to that object, is false relative to the specification of 9 as 'the number of the planets'. The attempt to attribute necessary properties to objects *an sich* aborts into nonsense. Quantification *abstracts* from the mode in which objects are designated. $(\exists x)F(x)$ is true or false according to whether or not at least one object satisfies the open sentence following the quantifier; but whether or not an object satisfies an open sentence is quite independent of how we refer to it or even of our having the linguistic means to refer to it at all. Thus there is a fundamental conflict between modality and quantification.

The only (dim) hope for modal logic, Quine thinks, lies in a reversion to "Aristotelian essentialism." He explains:

This means adopting an invidious attitude toward certain ways of uniquely specifying x, for example ['there are x planets'], and favoring other ways, for example [18], as somehow better revealing the "essence" of the object. Consequences of [18] can, from such a point of view, be looked upon as necessarily true of the object which is 9 (and is the number of the planets), while some consequences of ['there are x planets'] are rated still as only contingently true of that object. [Quine, [R&M], p. 155]

What is required of "Aristotelian essentialism" is that, despite examples like (3) and (4), it provides a sense for the idea of an object, *an sich* and by any name (or none), having some of its properties necessarily and some contingently, regardless of the fact that the former properties follow analytically for that object from certain modes of specifying it, just as the latter properties do from other modes of specification. Quantification in modal contexts must—on pain of not really being quantification at all—receive an interpretation that abstracts from the ways in which the values of variables are designated. The mixing of quantifiers and modal concepts thus effects a certain extensionalizing of the latter. How this occurs and is to be understood, it is the task of the attendant essentialism to explain.

Let us elaborate a bit the extensionalizing of modality that quantification effects. The principle of the indiscernibility of identicals states

(19) $x = y \supset_{x,y} . \, F(x) \supset F(y)$,

and we have, as modal principles concerning identity,

(20) $(x)\Box x = x$, and (20') $(x)\sim\Diamond x \neq x$.

By substitution into (19) we obtain

(21) $x = y \supset_{xy} . \, \Box(x = x) \supset \Box(x = y)$.

(20) and (21) then yield

(22) $x = y \supset_{xy} . \, \Box x = y$.

By a standard principle of modal logic, which is surely analytic of the concept of necessity, $\Box A \supset A$ for any well-formed formula A. From this and (22), together with quantifier laws, follows

(23) $x = y . \equiv_{xy} . \, \Box x = y$,

which expresses a partial collapse of modal distinctions for identity-contexts involving bound variables.

A somewhat parallel extensionalizing of belief has been presented by Church. By an elementary property of identity

(24) $\sim F(x) \supset_x . F(y) \supset_y x \neq y.$

By substitution into (24) we get

    (25)   For every x and every y, if George IV does not believe that $x \neq x$, then, if George IV believes that $x \neq y$, then $x \neq y$.

The first premiss,

    (26)   For every x, George IV does not believe that $x \neq x$,

is the analogue for belief of a substitution instance of (20′), and differs from it "in being no more than very likely rather than certain" (Church, "A Remark Concerning Quine's Paradox about Modality," forthcoming in *Sintaxis*, Montevideo). Now from (25) and (26) we obtain

    (27)   For every x and every y, if George IV believes that $x \neq y$, then $x \neq y$.

George IV's beliefs by (27) have a rather surprising power to control the facts, a power that Church concludes can be explained only on the doubtful assumption of what he calls "the principle of the transparency of belief." The principle is that belief applies to the satisfaction of conditions by objects entirely apart from the ways of specifying them (Church, ibid.). The transparency imposed on belief by quantification is the analogue of the essentialism required by quantified modal logic and is perhaps rather more counterintuitive.

    Church concludes,

> . . . Quine's objections, though strong, are no firm refutation of the Russellian resolution of the paradox. There may be those who, in the interest of the resolution of the paradox, are willing to accept both the complications about descriptions and the strange transparent notions of belief and necessity which result. And to them it can only be said that, well, it does seem strange. [Church, ibid.]

It is to be observed, once the element of justice in Quine's critique has been admitted, that the transparency of belief and necessity attendant on mixing these concepts with quantification does not rise above the level of free variables and primitive constants. The more usual nontransparent notions can also be expressed without paradox. Let $B(x, p)$ be used to mean that x believes that p; $S(x)$ that x scottizes; $W(x)$ that x is an author of *Waverley;* and $G(x)$ that x is George IV (or that x georgivizes). The Russellian may write

$$B((\imath x)G(x), (\imath x)S(x) \neq (\imath x)W(x))$$

to express the proposition, that George IV believes that Scott is not the author of *Waverley,* in its usual sense, which accords minimum scope to the contained descriptions. This does not entail

$$(\imath x)S(x) \neq (\imath x)W(x),$$

in spite of (27). Letting $N(x)$ mean that $x = 9$, (x nineizes), and letting $P(x)$ mean that x numbers the planets, the Russellian can express the contingent fact that

$$(\imath x)N(x) = (\imath x)P(x).$$

It does not follow from (23) that $\Box((\imath x)N(x) = (\imath x)P(x))$, in which again the descriptions have minimum scope [see Church, ibid.]. This entire sequence of considerations can be viewed by the Russellian as another vindication of his contention that definite descriptions are not proper names, logically speaking. They may even be taken as proof of this. It is the merit of Quine's critique to have raised a challenge, but it has not refuted quantified modality. In the words of Alonzo Church, which head this chapter, "What Quine has succeeded in demonstrating, it seems, is that his strictly extensionalist preferences have the effect of completely excluding modal logic" (Church, [Postscript 1968]; my translation).

7

Kripke's Critique of Frege and Russell

Part 1

Kripke's extraordinarily influential essay "Naming and Necessity" presents an attack on what he calls "the classical logical tradition" concerning proper names. Kripke further identifies the view he is attacking as "the Russell-Frege view," thereby indicating his belief that, in the respects in which he opposes them, the theories of Russell and Frege about proper names do not importantly differ. Because of the influence and importance of Kripke's essay, Dummett, correctly, thought it essential that his book *Frege: Philosophy of Language*, intended as a sympathetic, though critical, account of Frege's doctrines, include a defense of Frege against Kripke's attack. This appears in the form of an appendix, added by Dummett after his book had gone to press. Dummett, in defending Frege, extends and develops some of Frege's ideas in very interesting ways, but he also, I believe, fails at times to appreciate the full force of Kripke's arguments. This controversy is an enlightening one, and in Part 1 of this chapter I will attempt to sort out the principal issues involved, presenting both Kripke's arguments and Dummett's responses. My aim will be to decide the issues between them. In order to defend my conclusions, I will present my own views on the issues that divide Kripke and Dummett. Kripke's arguments against Frege fall, rather naturally, into two groups: modal arguments and nonmodal arguments. I shall divide the discussion in Part 1 accordingly. In Part 2 of this chapter I present some criticisms of Kripke that are quite independent of his controversy with Dummett.

I

The principal thesis of Kripke's attack on the classical logical tradition concerning proper names is that they lack Fregean sense. In this Kripke is consciously siding with John Stuart Mill, who held that, though "common names"—such as 'cow', 'man', and 'gold'—have both denotation and connotation, proper names—such as 'Plato' and 'London'—have denotation only. Kripke, as we will see, thinks that Mill was wrong about common names, for Kripke thinks that they too lack connotation and have denotation only. Mill's view about proper names is that they refer directly and that reference, for them, is not routed through their meaning or connotation, as is the case for common names. A view like Mill's was also held by Russell, not for ordinary proper names, but for a special category of singular terms: the "logically proper" names. Russell's logically proper names refer directly; and ordinary proper names do not, for him, refer at all, since they are disguised definite descriptions, which disappear when the propositions in whose "verbal expression" they occur are displayed in their correct logical form. While Russell would assimilate ordinary proper names to definite descriptions, Kripke would assimilate them to Russell's logically proper names.

Kripke's arguments against the "Russell-Frege" view are arguments against this description-theory of names. He does not, of course, attribute to Frege Russell's view that ordinary proper names are disguised or "truncated" definite descriptions. Yet he thinks his arguments against Russell's description-theory are also arguments against Frege's sense-theory, because he assumes that, if names have sense, their sense is always the same as that of some definite description. In this assumption Kripke is supported, perhaps, by this early footnote in Frege's essay "On Sense and Reference":

In the case of an actual proper name such as 'Aristotle' opinions as to the sense may differ. It might, for instance, be taken to be the following: the pupil of Plato and teacher of Alexander the Great. Anybody who does this will attach another sense to the sentence 'Aristotle was born in Stagira' than will a man who takes as the sense of the name: the teacher of Alexander the Great who was born in Stagira. So long as the reference remains the same, such variations of sense may be tolerated, although they are to be avoided in the theoretical structure of a demonstrative science and ought not to occur in a perfect language. [Frege, [SR], p. 58]

Frege here acknowledges that, in natural languages, proper names may have different senses for different speakers, and in illustrating the point he is led to state, in a particular case, what such alternative senses might be. It is hard to see how, in doing this, he could have done other than offer a pair of definite descriptions expressing the alternative senses. But it will not at all fit with Frege's views to suppose, as Kripke does, that every proper name has a sense that can appropriately be represented in this way. Indeed, Kripke's arguments against the description-theory seem to me to amount to a proof that, if proper names have sense, their sense cannot, characteristically, be expressed by definite descriptions of the kind used by Frege in the cited footnote. I say "characteristically" because I do not wish to deny that one might simply *stipulate*, for example, by definition, that some name is to have the sense of some definite description. But then I would say that this name *is* a description in accordance with its definition. Dummett claims, I think correctly, that, once we distinguish Frege's sense-theory from Russell's description-theory, we see that most of Frege's theory is unaffected by Kripke's attack. "What is important about Frege's theory," Dummett says, "is that a proper name, if it is to be considered as having a determinate sense, must have associated with it a specific criterion for recognizing a given object as the referent of the name; the referent of the name, if any, is whatever object satisfies that criterion" (Dummett, [*Frege*], p. 110). There is no requirement that this criterion be capable of being conveyed by means of a definite description of the kinds used by Frege in the note and by Kripke in his critique. For Frege, names identical in sense must be intersubstitutive even in belief-contexts without change of truth-value. Now try to think of a description of this kind that can replace the name 'Aristotle' in this way, *salva veritate!* (We can, in fact, always manufacture a description that trivially has the same sense as any name, as Quine has shown. For example, the sense of 'Socrates' is the same as 'the socratizer' where '*x* socratizes' is a predicate uniquely satisfiable only by Socrates.

This device has played a significant role in giving a Russellian account of the issues that concern us in this book. Here it suffices to observe that it is not against such descriptions that Kripke principally directs his attack. They should simply be set aside for the purpose of the present discussion.)

From Kripke's point of view, the theory that Wittgenstein presents in *Philosophical Investigations* does not differ significantly from Russell's and Frege's and is subject to essentially the same objections. For Wittgenstein the sense of a name such as 'Moses' is not given by a single specific criterion of identification but by a cluster of them. If we find that these criteria do not select a unique referent, we are prepared to drop some of them. We would not abandon the name 'Moses' if we were to discover, for example, that he did not lead the Israelites out of Egypt. But the referent of a name must satisfy *most*, even if not all, of these criteria; at least it must satisfy some central core of them.

A main point of Dummett's reply to Kripke is, as we have said, that Frege's theory is not the description-theory of names (Dummett, [*Frege*], p. 110). The reader is therefore surprised to find that a great deal of what follows is, nevertheless, a defense of the description-theory against Kripke's criticisms, for Dummett believes that if Kripke's arguments against Russell are successful they do refute Frege's theory. He explains why, in a passage I shall quote here but not discuss until later: ". . . it remains that it is essential to Frege's account that the sense of a proper name can be that of a definite description, and will be so for any proper name that is introduced by means of a definite description: hence, if the argument had worked, it would have been a flat refutation of Frege's account" (Dummett, ibid., p. 135).

II

Kripke agrees with Frege that proper names are first introduced into the language by associating with them a criterion of identification for their referents. But he holds that this criterion serves only to "fix the reference" of the name, not to fix its sense. Nothing does that, since, for Kripke, names do not have sense. If I introduce the name 'Aristotle' to you with the decription, 'the teacher of Alexander', then, according to Kripke, 'Aristotle' does not mean the same as 'the teacher of Alexander'; that description *fixes only the reference* of the name. In fact, for Kripke, the description-theory of names rests largely on this confusion between fixing the meaning and fixing the reference of names. It is not in general the case that the means initially employed to fix the reference of a name continues to determine its reference. For the present discussion we can concentrate on the case in which a name is introduced by means of a definite description and examine some of Kripke's arguments that aim to show that the description cannot be taken to be synonymous—identical in sense—with the name. Dummett takes as such an example the name 'St. Anne', because practically nothing is known of her except that she was the mother of Mary. "The reference of 'St. Anne' can therefore be taken as fixed in essentially only one way, namely by means of the description 'the mother of the Blessed Virgin Mary' " (Dummett, [*Frege*], p. 112). Kripke claims that there is a radical difference between names and descriptions such that a name cannot have the same sense as a definite description. This radical difference concerns their behavior in modal contexts. We shall now consider Kripke's arguments as applied to Dummett's example.

The name 'St. Anne' cannot be synonymous with the description 'the mother of Mary' because, says Kripke, the sentence 'The mother of Mary was a parent' expresses a necessary truth, but the sentence 'St. Anne was a parent' expresses a contingent truth. St. Anne, after all, might have died in infancy, or she might have remained a virgin all her life and never have become a parent. It is a purely contingent fact that she became a parent. Thus it follows that 'St. Anne' is not identical in meaning with 'the mother of Mary' even though that name was in fact (let us suppose) introduced to us only by the use of that description.

Now, of course, it is not exactly correct to say 'The mother of Mary could not but have been a parent', because she might not have existed at all. It is not true that the mother of Mary is a parent in every possible world, because there are possible worlds in which there is no such person; and in those worlds the sentence 'The mother of Mary is a parent' is certainly not true. But this objection does not really deal with Kripke's argument. It requires only a somewhat more careful formulation of it, which Dummett proceeds to give. The sentence 'The mother of Mary was necessarily a parent' is true if it is taken to mean 'It is necessarily true that, if there was such a person as Mary, and there was one and only one woman who was her mother, then that woman was a parent'. It is not, however, true to say 'St. Anne was necessarily a parent', meaning by this 'It is necessarily true that, if there was such a woman as St. Anne, then she was a parent'. It is only a contingent fact about St. Anne that she was a parent. Therefore, 'St. Anne' and 'the mother of Mary' cannot have the same sense.

In reply, Dummett points out that there is, after all, a sense in which it is true to say, 'St. Anne cannot but have been a parent', meaning 'If there was such a woman as St. Anne, then she could only have been a parent'. This flatly contradicts Kripke's claim that this sentence is not true, but Dummett argues that Kripke himself is committed to its truth. Kripke maintains that the sentence 'The Standard Meter Bar is one meter long' is an *a priori* truth. He holds this because he supposes that the term 'one meter' has its reference fixed by someone pointing to the Standard Meter Bar and introducing the term ostensively with the words 'By the length 'one meter' I shall mean the length of that bar'. Let us assume further that the term 'the Standard Meter Bar' is itself introduced ostensively by the words 'By 'the Standard Meter Bar' I shall mean that bar'. If that is how these terms are introduced to me, I cannot fail to know that the Standard Meter Bar is one meter long. This follows immediately for me from the very manner in which these terms had their references fixed. I cannot have understood this if I am so confused as to suppose that it is now an empirical question as to whether or not that bar really is one meter long. Thus, for me, the sentence 'The Standard Meter Bar cannot but be a meter long' is true. (More accurately, what is true is the assertion 'If the Standard Meter Bar exists, it cannot but be one meter long'.) Hence, Dummett argues, Kripke must grant the same for any name for which there is something specific—as there is for 'St. Anne'—that may be taken as fixing the reference.

So we have both 'The mother of Mary, if she exists, cannot but have been a parent' ('The mother of Mary, if she exists, is necessarily a parent') and 'St. Anne, if she exists, cannot but have been a parent' ('St. Anne, if she exists, is necessarily a parent'). We must also, it would seem, agree to this: 'St. Anne, if she exists, might not have been a parent' (she might have died in infancy). But, in some sense, 'The mother of Mary, if she exists, might not have been a parent' is also true. We seem to be confronting an ambiguity in modal contexts, and it is the same ambiguity for contexts containing proper names as for those containing definite descriptions. So far, according to Dummett, we have a case for assimilating names to definite descriptions on the score of their behavior in modal contexts but no case, *pace* Kripke, for distinguishing between them on this score.

For contexts containing definite descriptions, this ambiguity is readily accounted for in Russell's theory. What we are dealing with is the distinction between *de dicto* interpretations of statements containing modal operators and *de re* interpretations. This distinction, for the simple cases we are considering, can be represented as a matter of contrasting scopes accorded definite descriptions in modal contexts. A more accurate account of the matter requires that the contingency of existence be recognized; i.e., the opposed interpretations should be represented as presenting a contrast between the *de dicto*,

$$\Box[(\imath x)(\phi x)]\mathrm{E}!(\imath x)(Mx) \supset . \, P(\imath x)(Mx),$$

and the *de re*,

$$\mathrm{E}!(\imath x)(Mx) \supset . \, [(\imath x)(Mx)]\Box P(\imath x)(Mx).$$

It is in the *de dicto* sense, in which the description is taken as falling within the scope of 'necessarily', that our sentence 'The mother of Mary, if she exists, is necessarily a parent' is true, and it is in the *de re* sense, in which the scopes of the modal operator and the description are reversed, that our sentence is false.

Now, Dummett argues, proper names induce the same ambiguities of scope in modal contexts as do descriptions. Notice, first, that even in fully extensional contexts we must acknowledge scope distinctions for proper names as much as for descriptions once we see that the truth-value of a sentence containing a proper name is affected if that name lacks a referent. Take, for example, 'Vulcan', the name of the nonexistent planet whose orbit was for some time wrongly supposed to lie within that of Mercury. Now consider the sentence 'Vulcan orbits around the sun'. I think it quite reasonable to say, with Frege, that this sentence simply lacks a truth-value because the name 'Vulcan' lacks a referent. One might, for the same reason, hold that the sentence is false. Or one might hold that the sentence is false because there is no other alternative to being true (and our sentence is surely not true). What then of the sentence, 'Vulcan does not orbit the sun'? Since it contains the same nondenoting name, it seems, on the one hand, that it should be regarded as either false or without truth-value, just as was the sentence in the positive form. How then can we form the latter's contradictory? There is a clear intuition that, since Vulcan does not exist, it is true to say, 'It is not the case that Vulcan orbits the sun'.

We seem to be dealing here with the same ambiguity that arises for descriptions that fail to denote anything, and it seems equally plausible to deal with it similarly by invoking the idea of the scope of the name. We might introduce a scope operator for names and distinguish one case in which the scope of the name lies within the sign of negation thus,

$$\sim[v]S(v).$$

We might read this as 'It is not the case that Vulcan orbits the sun' and hold it true because the negated sentence is either false or without a truth-value. We would then represent the case in which these scopes are reversed thus,

$$[v]\sim S(v),$$

to be read, perhaps, as 'Vulcan does not orbit the sun', and regard it as either false or without truth-value, just as is the nonnegated form. Russell, of course, has no use for a scope-distinguisher for proper names, but that is because his logically proper names are guaranteed a referent.

Hence, Dummett claims, in a description-theory of names, such as Russell's, there is no difficulty in accounting for Kripke's observations. Names, in this theory, are descriptions and hence induce scope ambiguity in modal contexts. But even if one does not adopt Russell's description-theory, one can, says Dummett, account for the ambiguity in terms of scope. We have already seen how this works for names in extensional contexts. Let us now consider the modal cases. 'St. Anne could not but have been a mother' ('St. Anne is necessarily a mother') exhibits the same scope ambiguity we found above in this sentence, with the description 'the mother of Mary' in the place of 'St. Anne'. We again have the same contrast between the *de dicto* interpretation,

$$\Box[s]M(s),$$

and the *de re,*

$$[s]\Box M(s).$$

In the more accurate interpretation we can utilize Russell's singular existence-predicate 'E!' to represent the contrasting interpretations thus:

$$\Box[s] \,.\, E!(s) \supset M(s) \qquad \textit{de dicto,}$$

and

$$E!(s) \supset .\, [s]\Box M(s) \qquad \textit{de re.}$$

The above observations could have been made in defense of the thesis that names are descriptions. But that is not Dummett's aim. He advocates a theory that treats names as an irreducible semantic and syntactic category but offers a uniform explanation (scope ambiguity) of what appears to be just the same phenomenon. Kripke, on the other hand, while accepting the scope explanation for definite descriptions, wants to give an entirely different account for proper names. He acknowledges no role for the notion of scope for proper names at all. Kripke explains the ambiguity we are concerned with as arising rather from different modal notions. He distinguishes between metaphysical and epistemological concepts of necessity and possibility. The sense in which 'The Standard Meter Bar could not but be one meter long' and 'St. Anne could not but be a parent' are true is, according to Kripke, an epistemic sense. We know these truths *a priori*. It is knowledge grasped solely in virtue of the way the words are used, that is, from the fact that the term 'one meter' was introduced by having its reference fixed by pointing to a bar and saying 'That is the Standard Meter Bar'. The name 'St. Anne' was introduced by having its reference fixed by the words 'St. Anne was the mother of Mary'. Because of this I cannot consider it an empirical question to be determined *a posteriori* whether or not these statements are true. No empirical investigation could falsify them. We know them *a priori*. On the other hand, both statements are metaphysically contingent, since obviously St. Anne might never have become a mother, and that bar might have been broken in half, in which case it would not have been one meter long.

So, in Kripke's view, definite descriptions induce scope ambiguities in modal contexts. I assume that he would agree with Dummett that proper names, as well as descriptions, induce scope ambiguities in extensional contexts because failure of a name or of a description to have a referent affects the truth-value of sentences containing these terms. But Kripke certainly wants to deny that the truth-value of either a modal or an extensional sentence containing a denoting proper name can vary according to the scope of the name. Kripke accounts for this difference between names and descriptions as arising because names are all "rigid designators" and descriptions, generally, are not. Again, for Kripke descriptions have a sense, and names do not. To say that a designator is *rigid* is to say that it denotes the same thing at all possible worlds. 'Nixon', for example, denotes Nixon at all possible worlds. It does not follow from this that Nixon exists in all possible worlds. In that case 'Nixon' would be what Kripke calls a "strongly rigid" designator. We can compare, for example, the name 'Benjamin Franklin' with the description 'the inventor of bifocals'. In the actual world the inventor of bifocals is Benjamin Franklin; but in some other possible world the inventor of bifocals is someone else or perhaps no one, since it is a purely contingent fact that Franklin rather than someone else invented them and that they were invented at all. But there is no possible world in which Franklin is not Franklin. Thus we can say 'Franklin might not have been the inventor of bifocals' and mean by this that there is a possible world in which the person who satisfies the description is not, as in the actual world, Franklin. But we cannot say 'Franklin might not have been Franklin', for 'Franklin' is a rigid designator and

127

so designates the same thing at every possible world. Here, along with Kripke, I think we have a conclusive argument against treating names as descriptions. Since there is a sense in which it is true to say 'Nixon might not have been the winner of the 1968 presidential election', but no sense in which it is true to say 'Nixon might not have been Nixon', 'Nixon' cannot have the same sense as 'the winner of the 1968 presidential election'. Nor, for similar reasons, as Kripke maintains, can the name 'Nixon' have the same sense as any other nonrigid definite description.

Kripke accounts for this difference by appeal to the circumstance that names are rigid designators, and in this he has exposed an important feature of the logic of proper names. But then, the scope difference that Dummett thinks he finds for names in modal contexts must be illusory. There cannot be a difference in truth-value between (1) 'Necessarily St. Anne is a parent', $\Box[s]P(s)$, and (2) 'St. Anne is necessarily a parent', $[s]\Box P(s)$. Dummett holds that the first of these is true and the second false. But the first of these is true only if 'St. Anne' designates a parent at every possible world, and the second is false only if the person designated by 'St. Anne' at the actual world is not a parent at some possible world. Thus we can have both (1) true and (2) false only if 'St. Anne' does not designate the same thing at all possible worlds, that is, if it is not a rigid designator. But, to repeat, if 'St. Anne' does not designate rigidly—if it designates different things at different possible worlds—there is a sense in which 'St. Anne might not be St. Anne' is true, just as there is a sense in which 'St. Anne might not have been the mother of Mary' is true.

Now, surprisingly, Dummett seems to concede all of this in the end, for he says,

> We are now in a position to understand the grain of truth in Kripke's doctrine of proper names as rigid designators. For modal contexts in general, there is no relevant difference between proper names and definite descriptions: but the matter stands otherwise when the name of the description is preceded by the verb 'to be' or 'to become'. We may intelligibly say that the mother of Mary might never have become a parent, or even, at a pinch, that the mother of Mary might not have been the mother of Mary; but we cannot say that St. Anne might not have been St. Anne, and, if we say that the mother of Mary

might not have been St. Anne, it is still the definite description, and not the name, which lies within the scope of the modal operator, just as when we say that St. Anne might not have been the mother of Mary (though the two statements are not equivalent). [Dummett, [*Frege*], p. 131]

The position thus characterized is actually incoherent, for what Dummett says is just a "grain of truth" in Kripke's position is much more than that. It is closer to the facts to say that what Dummett is conceding is Kripke's whole position. If we cannot say 'St. Anne might not have been St. Anne', this is because this name does not induce the scope ambiguities in modal contexts on which Dummett insists, and this in turn refutes his claim that "For modal contexts in general there is no relevant difference between proper names and definite descriptions."

I conclude that Kripke has established his case that names and descriptions behave differently in modal contexts. Consequently, it must be conceded that these arguments refute what is usually thought of as the description-theory of names. (Remember that we have excluded from the present discussion Quine's description 'the nixonizer'. None of Kripke's arguments work against this description as the equivalent of 'Nixon'. Just as there is no sense in which Nixon might not have been Nixon, so is there no sense in which the nixonizer might not have been the nixonizer. It is false *de dicto* that it might have been the case that the winner of the 1968 presidential election did not win the 1968 election, but it is true *de dicto* that Nixon might not have won the 1968 presidential election. But it is also true *de dicto* that it might have been the case that the nixonizer did not win the 1968 presidential election. So 'Nixon' behaves just like the Quineian description 'the nixonizer' in modal contexts. The reason for this is that, unlike 'the winner of the 1968 presidential election', both 'Nixon' and 'the nixonizer' are rigid designators.) But the thesis of Kripke's that mainly concerned us is that ordinary proper names do not have sense, and that thesis is not established by these arguments. What Kripke's arguments show is that, if names do have sense, their sense cannot be the same as such ordinary descriptions as 'the winner of the 1968 election' or 'the inventor of bifocals'.

From this point of view, the whole strategy that Dummett is following seems curiously ill-conceived. He could have conceded all of Kripke's arguments about the differences in behavior in modal contexts of names and descriptions and observed that, though they are destructive of Russell's view, they miss their mark when directed at Frege. The explanation for this state of affairs is that Dummett insists on defending the description-theory because he has convinced himself that Frege really is committed to a form of it. Why he believes this he explains as follows:

> If the objection treated [above] could have been sustained, it would have shown definitely that the sense of a proper name can never be identical with that of a definite description. Admittedly, we rejected Kripke's claim that Frege believed such an identity to hold in the case of every proper name; it remains that it is essential to Frege's account that the sense of a proper name can be that of a definite description, and will be so for any proper name that is introduced by means of a definite description: hence, if the argument had worked, it would have been a flat refutation of Frege's account. [Dummett, [*Frege*], p. 135]

What Dummett here maintains is that a proper name will, if introduced by means of a definite description, necessarily acquire the sense of the description in the process. Further, proper names can always be so introduced. The point is important because, if Dummett is correct about this, Kripke's arguments against the description-theory really do refute Frege's sense-theory. However, I believe that Dummett is not right. He gives no argument for his view, and we must assume that that is because he regards the matter as self-evident: after all, to introduce a new name into the language is to give it both a sense and (thereby) a reference, so it would seem that this newly acquired sense must be that of the introducing description if it is introduced by means of a description. But this, I think, is wrong. A name can be successfully introduced, by whatever means, only if, as Wittgenstein observed, a great deal of stage-setting is already in place—only if a great deal of language is already understood. Just try to explain the name 'St. Anne' to a child who does not yet understand what even a name is! One succeeds in introducing a new name only if it is understood that what is being introduced is a *proper name* as opposed, say, to a title, a predicate, or an expression of some other semantic category; in other words, the person to whom the proper name is introduced must already have the concept of a proper name, and some knowledge of the way expressions of this category work, if the "introduction" is to be other than an idle ceremony. It is a feature of the sense of a singular term that it is a proper name, as Dummett himself observes: "An expression's belonging to the category of proper names is a feature of its sense: and we ought to be able to say with what aspect of its sense this feature is connected" (ibid., p. 55). Similarly, an expression's belonging to the category of definite descriptions is a feature of its sense. With respect to these features, any proper name will differ in sense from any ordinary description. For example, it is a feature of the sense of 'St. Anne' that the truth-value of a simple modal sentence containing that name is the same whether the name is taken as falling within the scope of the modality or outside its scope. A name introduced by means of an ordinary description acquires only part of its sense in the process. The feature of its sense that it has in virtue of its mere membership in the category of proper names is something it must already be understood to possess if the intended introduction is to succeed. I conclude that Dummett need not have attempted to refute Kripke's attack on the description-theory in order to defend Frege's sense-theory of names. Kripke's attack on the description-theory is successful, and his thesis that proper names are rigid designators is correct. But Kripke's arguments, as thus far presented, do not undermine the sense-theory. We have considered only some of his arguments—the modal arguments. Before going on to consider Kripke's nonmodal arguments I will present some positive considerations in favor of the sense-theory of names.

What is learned when one acquires a name? Consider this simple situation: A father points to Venus in the early evening and says to his son, 'That planet is Hesperus'. Let us suppose that the child has never heard the name before or that, if he has, he has not previously known what it named. Under normal circumstances the child can now use the name himself; he has acquired it. This capacity is exhibited, for example, when, on a subsequent occasion, he himself says, 'There is Hesperus again'. His ability to apply the name again on another occasion is an exercise of his capacity to recognize the planet in altered circumstances. Thus, part of what was acquired is a criterion of identification of the referent of the name, and this is what

Frege means by its sense. Consider the same child on another occasion in another time of the year. This time his father points to Venus in the early morning and explains to his son, 'That planet is Phosphorus'. Again we may suppose that, as a result, the child acquires another criterion of identification for that heavenly body, so that, on other mornings, he can recognize it and call it 'Phosphorus' again. Obviously he need not realize that he is looking at the same planet that on any previous occasion he has identified as Hesperus. It can be an important discovery for him that Hesperus is Phosphorus. Frege introduced his distinction between sense and reference in the context of an attempt to answer the questions 'How can a true statement of identity ever be informative?' and 'What information does it convey?' In the present simplified case it is entirely clear what has been learned when the child learns that Hesperus is Phosphorus. What he has learned is that the criterion of identification associated with 'Hesperus', its sense, picks out the same object as is picked out by the criterion of identification associated with 'Phosphorus', *its* sense.

In this connection there are considerations of a more general methodological character that are relevant. My methodological standpoint is this: I wish to study and compare a number of alternative theories of meaning—those of Frege, Russell, and Kripke in particular. My aim is to determine which of these theories is the best—which accounts for all of the phenomena in the best way, and which offers the best explanation of such phenomena as the paradoxes involving intensional contexts. One of these theories, Frege's, requires the ascription of atomic senses to the prime constants—proper names—of a language. There is no way in which Frege's theory of meaning can operate without such atomic senses or individual concepts. Consider these sentences: 'Moses was a Jew' and 'Socrates was a Jew'. They differ in truth-value, hence they express different thoughts or propositions. The thoughts are the senses of the sentences, and each thought is a function of the senses of the constituent names contained in the sentence that expresses it. Since the other constituent names are the same (and are in the same order) in both sentences, it follows that the difference between the two propositions is due entirely to the difference between the senses of the two names 'Socrates' and 'Moses'.

If, on examination, Frege's theory should appear to be the best available and also to be fully adequate, then, because the best theory demands it, we would have an excellent reason for ascribing sense to proper names. Because of such considerations, I think of senses as "theoretical entities," not available to immediate sensory observation. Nevertheless, it may be that they are available for some kind of nonsensory observation. Frege often speaks of senses as though he takes them to be real, objective constituents of reality, immediately grasped by the mind through the medium of language. It is this aspect of his thought that is referred to when his theory is called "platonistic." Alonzo Church defends this aspect of Frege's views in the following passage:

> To those who object to the introduction of abstract entities at all I would say that I believe that there are more important criteria by which a theory should be judged. The extreme demand for a simple prohibition of abstract entities under all circumstances perhaps arises from a desire to maintain the connection between theory and observation. But the preference of (say) *seeing* over *understanding* as a method of observation seems to me capricious. For just as an opaque body may be seen, so a concept may be understood or grasped. And the parallel between the two cases is indeed rather close. In both cases the observation is not direct but through intermediaries—light, lens of eye or optical instrument, and retina in the case of the visible body, linguistic expressions in the case of the concept. And in both cases there are or may be tenable theories according to which the entity in question, opaque body or concept, is not assumed, but only those things which would otherwise be called its effects. [Church, [NAESA], p. 442]

This is a point of view with which I am very sympathetic. We do understand what people say and write. There is such a thing as grasping or understanding concepts; and of course such concepts are not parts of the spatiotemporal world. To those who would reject them on this ground, I would say that their view is a mere prejudice and that there is more between heaven and earth than is contained in their philosophy. In defense of sense, I would say both that theory requires it and that observation (understanding) reveals it. It is not as though there is a brute fact of the matter: intensional entities either do or do not constitute part of "the ultimate furniture of the world." The point is rather that, if the best theory requires these entities, then that is the best argument for their reality. Again, if, according to the best available theory, we "grasp" senses in our use of language, then, from the point of view here advocated, we have the best reason we can have to conclude that we do possess this nonsensory mode of awareness of them.

III

The arguments of section II concerned the behavior of names in modal contexts. Not only is it the case that a description used to fix the reference of a name *might* not, in fact, be satisfied by the bearer of the name (Nixon might not have been the winner of the 1968 presidential election), but we may actually discover that it is not. For example, many people would explain the reference of the name 'Gödel' with the description 'the man who proved the incompleteness of arithmetic'. It is, however, entirely intelligible to us to suppose that we might discover that Gödel was an impostor who stole the proof from someone else—say, Schmidt. Then the sentence 'Gödel did not, in fact, discover the incompleteness of arithmetic' cannot mean 'The discoverer of the incompleteness of arithmetic did not, in fact, discover the incompleteness of arithmetic', nor, for similar reasons, can it have the same sense as any other ordinary definite description.

The difference between this argument and the one dealt with in section II is that there we were concerned with metaphysical possibility, while here the possibility is epistemic. What we are concerned with here is not the metaphysical possibility that Gödel might not have discovered the incompleteness of arithmetic because there is a possible world in which he does not make that discovery. Rather, our concern here is with an epistemic possibility concerning the real world. We might discover that we have all been mistaken in supposing that Gödel discovered the incompleteness of arithmetic.

In order to answer this, Dummett concludes that what is needed is a modification of Frege's theory (and Russell's) along Wittgensteinian lines. Wittgenstein observes that we do not use a name such as 'Moses' as though it were merely short for some one definite description, such as 'the man who led the Israelites out of Egypt', for we would not abandon the name if it should be discovered that there was no single leader who led the Israelites out of slavery but that the task was performed by a committee. Wittgenstein replaces a single sharp criterion of identification as the sense of a name with a cluster of alternatives of which we are prepared in advance to abandon any fairly small subset. Thus, as Dummett says, "What makes it possible to entertain the possibility that Gödel might be discovered not to have proved, or not to have been the first to prove, the incompleteness of arithmetic is the fact that there exist other generally accepted ways of determining the reference of the name 'Gödel' " (Dummett, [*Frege*], p. 136). It is as though a table were held up by a number of props. If one is knocked down, the others hold it up. Of course, if enough of these props are removed, our table will collapse.

With any widely used name that has been with us for a long time there will thus be a cluster of alternative criteria for identifying their bearers, and no one of them will have the privileged position of being *the* sense of the name since all of the others will convey additional information about the reference—information that is not entailed by the sense. From this point of view, Frege's picture of language, in which each term has its own unique sense, understood by all the users of the language, is seen by Dummett to be an idealized model of how language works rather than a naturalistic picture of that working. The model is nearly enough approximated in some cases. If, one day, I explain to a child who has never heard the name that Homer is the author of the *Iliad* and the *Odyssey,* I would not expect the child to know what to make of his brother's subsequent remark that these poems were not written by Homer but by another man. It is clear, in any case, that a language could actually function as the idealized model does. That, according to Dummett, is because the idealized model captures the essential mechanism underlying the use of language, however different that working would be represented to be in a naturalistic description.

Nevertheless, Dummett concedes that the observed deviations from the idealized model do threaten the credibility of Frege's theoretical account. Kripke's critique turns largely on exploiting these deviations. There has been a long tradition of opposition to the idea that proper names, and, in particular, personal proper names, are words like any others. They are sometimes said to be not genuine parts of the language at all but rather something in the nature of extralinguistic adjuncts to communication. To deny that they have meaning or sense is a partial articulation of this view, which is reinforced by the consideration that it is distinctively odd to speak of the "meanings" of names at all, unless in the sense in which 'Stalin' means 'steel'—a sense irrelevant to its functioning logically as a name. Again, the simplified example, given above, of the different senses attached to 'Hesperus' and 'Phosphorus' is possible only because we imagine ourselves able to recover the conditions under which these names were first introduced. For most names, the occasion and manner of introduction are long forgotten, and it is, in fact, impossible to draw clear lines between what is true in virtue of their sense and what is a matter of collateral information. A sharp distinction between analytic and synthetic cannot therefore be drawn.

Our loose and imprecise ways with language are generally of no great practical moment, but it can, on occasion, be important to abandon them. Suppose it to become a matter of some urgency to decide whether Moses or some other supposed historical figure ever actually existed. Then the situation with this name, as Wittgenstein describes it, is no longer tolerable. We would have to fix on some rather precise criterion of identification for Moses if the issue of his existence were to be intelligibly pursued. As we make our language, or some portion of it, more precise on such occasions, it comes closer and closer to Frege's idealized model, and in this way, says Dummett, the model itself is confirmed.

One way to see that proper names, including personal proper names, do function essentially as they are represented as doing in the idealized model that Frege constructed is to compare their use with the use of other words that would generally be acknowledged to possess a sense. To fully acquire a word such as 'table', it is essential to acquire the capacity to identify objects correctly as tables. The sense of the word just is the criterion of identification that is acquired in learning the word. A normal person's inability ever or even generally to distinguish between what is correctly called a 'table' and what is correctly called a 'chair' would be a conclusive reason for saying that the person had not mastered the meanings of these words. The situation is essentially the same with proper names. One has not fully acquired the name 'Nixon' if one is unable ever to use the name in an act of identification or if one continually calls Carter 'Nixon' and Nixon 'Carter'. If, when asked to find out whether Nixon is in the next room, I do not have the faintest idea whom to look for, I do not know the sense of the name, just as would be the case if, when asked to determine whether anything in the next room was what we call a 'table', I had not the faintest idea how to determine that.

What is special about personal proper names is that each person, or local group of persons, has its own special stock of them. I can expect to communicate effectively with any speakers of English, no matter how remote they may be from my local scene, but I may share only a relatively small number of personal proper names with them. This certainly points to an important feature of the logic of these names, and it is this feature of them that leads some to regard them as not genuinely part of the language. After all, the words of our language and their meanings are the shared possession of all who speak the language. But this view ceases to be plausible when we turn away from exclusive attention to personal proper names to consider proper names generally. The names 'Paris' and 'New York' are as widely shared, I suppose, as such words as 'birch' and 'elm', which are certainly words of our language. It is not reasonable to suppose that these names, 'Paris' and 'New York', function differently from more local possessions, such as the name of my favorite amaryllis plant. The sense of these names—what one knows when one understands them—is the criterion of identification of their referents.

IV

According to Frege, to understand a sentence is to grasp the thought it expresses. The sense of a complex expression is composed of the senses of its constituents. This, however, can be a correct account of the workings of only the idealized model of our language; for all of us frequently use names of which we can give no very good explanation, not because none exists, but because we do not know it. The examples Kripke uses are 'General Theory of Relativity' and 'Gödel's Theorem'. The same applies to names of species and to terms for natural kinds as well. There are times when we use words, and make quite adequate use of them, without attaching to them anything that can be considered a sense. I cannot tell the difference between a birch and an elm. About all I know is that these are names of large trees, and that is good enough for the present purposes I have concerning these words. If my friend tells me sadly that his beautiful birch has been killed by lightning, I will feel entirely free to give him my condolences without rushing off first to look up 'birch' in the dictionary. "In a great many such cases," says Dummett, "we are exploiting the fact, known to us, that the word we use is part of the common language" (*[Frege]*, p. 138). We intend our use to be responsible to the sense of the word that is the common possession of the speakers of our language. Understanding another person is not a matter of reading his mind. We operate on the assumption that it is our common language that is in use and that words have the sense publicly associated with them. Normally it does not matter at all that on some particular occasion a speaker—another or ourselves—has no very clear idea what that sense is. The purpose of communication is not thereby frustrated.

For some terms—for example, terms for natural kinds, such as 'hydrogen'—the common sense may be the possession of a group of experts. We use such terms with the intention that our use shall conform to that of these experts. Thus, Dummett urges us to view Frege's theory as an idealized model that requires much modification before it becomes a realistic picture; but it is an idealization that displays the "essential mechanism" of language, and it is one to which, for scientific purposes, we need constantly to try to approximate. The same qualifications of the simple model that applies to names applies to all other words as well. But this model "displays the only mechanism by which a name could acquire reference, even though the actual working has been simplified for the sake of perspicuity. It is not a choice between Frege's theory and some alternative theory: there is no other theory" (*[Frege]*, p. 143).

V

Kripke applies his notion of rigid designation to expressions not ordinarily thought of as proper names, e.g., 'meter'. Others are mass terms, such as 'water' and 'gold'; terms for physical phenomena, such as 'heat', 'light', and 'sound'; and words for kinds of organisms, such as 'cat' or 'ant'. For Frege, all of these, in certain of their uses, would count as proper names. Kripke's idea is that, just as proper names do not have sense, neither do any of the kinds of terms listed above. That they do not reveals itself in the fact that such terms do not apply on the basis of superficial appearances. What looks, tastes, smells, and feels like gold may not, in fact, be gold. Consider, for example, fool's gold. If creatures were found on Mars who from their bodily appearance looked exactly like men but did not share a common origin with men, they would not be men. To be gold, a substance must have a certain kind of atomic structure: it must have atomic number 79. The creatures on Mars are not *men* because they do not share a common origin, as the children of Adam, with the men of our planet.

What has this to do with the issue over the legitimacy of the notion of sense? It does bring out an important consideration: "Meanings are not in the head" (Putnam, [MM], p. 139). Something can look, taste, smell, feel, and sound just like Richard Nixon and not be Richard Nixon. We could discover this by cutting him (it) open and finding that, instead of muscle and bone and blood, what was inside was just lots of metal wheels and cogs. *That* is not Nixon! *Second:* We may use a technical or scientific term with the intention of being responsible to the sense attributed to it by a group of experts. Putnam calls this the "division-of-labor principle" in semantics (ibid., p. 144). I can use a term, say 'aspirin', without knowing anything more about it than that it is an analgesic drug, but I can still use it with the intention of making my use responsible to that of the experts who do know the chemical composition of the stuff. Sense is a community possession. Frege tends to regard any difference in sense between two speakers as a difference in ideolect. On such a view, a language itself becomes a mere collection of ideolects. On the ground of the present observations, Dummett is urging a modification of Frege's strict view, a modification that would make sense the collective possession of all the speakers of a language. Thus I can use words whose sense I grasp only partially, or even mistakenly, in successful communication because I can depend on being understood to intend their commonly accepted sense, however deviant my own use may be.

There is another meaning that can be given to the words "sense is not in the head"; it concerns the relation between theory and observation. In this meaning, these words express an objection to a certain kind of crude empiricism that is sometimes used in discussions of the topics we are dealing with in this study. For example, in connection with his arguments against Russell's description-theory of proper names, Kripke seems to argue as follows. According to this theory, the common users of a proper name associate with it some particular, unique description that conveys its sense. (We need not, for present purposes, distinguish between Russell's theory and Frege's.) He then argues against this by means of a kind of thought-experiment. Kripke asks us to consider what our neighbor might say if we asked him, e.g., "Who is Albert Einstein?" Assuming our neighbors to be ordinary folk, not educated in physics, we might get such answers as "the inventor of the atom bomb" or just "a great scientist." The requisite unique description or sense seems just not to be there. Kripke's assumption seems to be that, if names have a definite sense for us, we ought to be able somehow to verify this by introspecting the contents of our own minds or by examining the results of others' carrying out such introspection. The assumption seems to be that, if we attach a definite sense to the proper names we use, we ought to be able to verify by introspection that we do. But I would protest against this method of direct verification that I would not know what a sense "looked like" if I did happen to see it by introspection. The theory, of course, requires verification. But such verification should be made by confronting the theory with all of our relevant linguistic behavior—not with the contents we find by introspection to be present or not present in our own minds.

Part 2

Kripke's main thesis about proper names is that they are rigid designators. The thesis is recommended as having an immediate intuitive appeal, and certainly not as a consequence of considerations about scope ambiguities in modal contexts. The intuition is this: We are able to use ordinary proper names to describe all kinds of counterfactual situations in which the things named do not have any of the properties ordinarily used in describing them and for picking them out in the actual world. We can consider situations in which, e.g., Aristotle is not a student of Plato, not the author of the *Organon,* not the teacher of Alexander, and so on through all of the well-known properties commonly associated with him. Still, it is to *Aristotle* we are referring. If 'Aristotle' were synonymous with 'the teacher of Alexander', Kripke asks, how could we make sense of a situation in which we suppose that Aristotle never taught anybody? That would be to suppose that the teacher of Alexander was not a teacher, and that is absurd. Still, we can perfectly well suppose that *Aristotle* never went into teaching. This is just to say that 'Aristotle' designates rigidly the same person in every counterfactual situation no matter how different Aristotle, in that situation, is supposed to be from the Aristotle of this world. Any attempt to replace these considerations by observations about scope distinctions for proper names in modal contexts is misguided because it loses sight of this guiding intuition. (See Kripke's Preface to *Naming and Necessity.*)

The intuition that proper names designate the same things in every counterfactual situation—that they designate rigidly—supports, and in turn is supported by, the consideration that true statements of identity, such as 'Hesperus = Phosphorus', are necessary truths. For that 'Hesperus = Phosphorus' is a necessary truth just means that it is true in every counterfactual situation (every possible world). Thus, supposing 'Hesperus = Phosphorus' to be true is supposing these two names to denote the same thing in this world. And supposing these names to denote rigidly is just supposing that they denote the same thing in all possible worlds, i.e., 'Hesperus = Phosphorus' is a necessary truth. This intuition is indeed very strong, for what would a possible world be like in which Hesperus (i.e., Phosphorus) was not Phosphorus? It would be a world in which Hesperus was not self-identical—an impossible situation.

It is then a consequence of the thesis that proper names are rigid designators that codesignative proper names are intersubstitutive, *salva veritate,* in modal contexts. We thus arrive at a solution to one form of the puzzle that has been supposed by Quine and others to stand in the way of a clear interpretation of modality. From the truth of

(1) Hesperus = Phosphorus

and

(2) $\Box(\text{Hesperus} = \text{Hesperus})$,

we seem able to infer the false statement

(3) $\Box$(Hesperus = Phosphorus),

by the replacement of equals for equals, using Leibniz's Law.

Kripke solves this form of the puzzle involving proper names by maintaining that indeed codesignating proper names are intersubstitutive in modal contexts. Hence (3) *is* true, not false. He goes on to explain that the reason (3) is supposed to be false is that (1) is an *a posteriori,* not an *a priori,* truth. If we suppose that no *a posteriori* truth can be necessary, we will be unable to accept (3) as true. But, Kripke maintains, this supposition is just a piece of unsupported dogmatism and perhaps just a confusion of metaphysical and epistemic modalities. At any rate, no adequate reason has ever been given for accepting it.

Now Kripke goes on to argue that the reason names succeed in designating rigidly is precisely because they lack Fregean senses. If 'Aristotle' had the same sense as 'the teacher of Alexander', we could not, coherently, consider a counterfactual situation in which Aristotle was not a teacher, and so on for all of the alternative candidates one might wish to propose as the sense of this name. It would then seem that it is for this same reason—that names lack sense—that codesignative names are intersubstitutive in modal contexts. For what else might cause sentences (2) and (3), above, to have *different* truth-values except a difference in sense of the two names, 'Hesperus' and 'Phosphorus'?

Now the following question arises: Has not Kripke's successful treatment of this puzzle about Hesperus and Phosphorus in the context of modality only increased the difficulties involved in dealing with the other puzzles that any adequate theory of naming ought to be able to deal with? In particular, how can we now deal with another puzzle just like this one, except that the relevant modality is not necessity, but belief? Consider,

(4)   Hesperus = Phosphorus,

and suppose it true that,

(5)   Jones believes that Hesperus = Hesperus,

where the truth of (5) entails no more than that Jones has the use of the name involved. Still, we might suppose Jones to be ignorant of (4), so that it is false that

(6)   Jones believes that Hesperus = Phosphorus.

Now Frege devised the concept of sense precisely to explain such paradoxical situations. 'Hesperus' and 'Phosphorus' are not inter-substitutive in belief-contexts because, though they agree in reference, they differ in sense. But Kripke's arguments seem to show that *because* names lack sense they are substitutive in modal contexts. He uses the fact of rigidity to support his rejection of sense for proper names. How then can he explain the failure of substitutivity of codesignative names in belief-contexts? Surely Kripke cannot argue that (6) is in fact true and that our conviction of its falsity is based on confusion of modalities; for no one would argue that a statement of belief such as (6) cannot be true because (4) is an *a posteriori* truth.

When Kripke takes up these questions in a subsequent paper (Kripke, "A Puzzle about Belief" [PAB]), his strategy, in fact, is to challenge the claim that proper names are not intersubstitutive, when coreferential, in belief-contexts. He claims, rather, that here we are in a "paradoxical area" in which a number of other principles—disquotation, principles of translation—are equally involved; and he claims that it is still an open question whether belief-contexts are "Shakespearean" or not (that is, whether or not they admit substitutivity for coreferential proper names as a valid mode of inference). At any rate, Kripke offers no solution to this form of the puzzle about substitutivity.

The puzzle about belief that Kripke presents in this paper is this. Suppose Pietro is a normal, native speaker of Italian who lives in Italy and speaks not a word of English or any other language except Italian. He has read about England and its capital city, and, on the basis of this reading and of pictures he has seen and things he has heard, he constantly expresses a wish to see this city. He says such things as 'Londra è bella', and he behaves in such a way as to lead his Italian acquaintances to say unhesitatingly:

(7)   Pietro creda che Londra è bella.

Now suppose that Pietro moves to England and, in fact, takes up residence in London. His home is in a poor and unattractive part of the city. None of his neighbors speaks any language except English, and he learns English directly from those around him, just as native speakers do. He learns that the name of his city in English is 'London', and he begins to say such things as 'London is ugly' and to behave in such a way as to lead English-speakers who know him to say, unhesitatingly,

(8) Pietro believes that London is not beautiful.

Of course it never occurs to Pietro that the city he calls 'Londra' when he is speaking Italian is the same as the city he calls 'London' when he is speaking English, and no one informs him of this. Kripke's question is this: Does he or does he not believe that London is beautiful? There is a strong temptation to say, on the basis of (7) and (8) that Pietro's beliefs are inconsistent: that he believes both that London is beautiful and that London is not beautiful. Against this conclusion, however, is the consideration that, if a person has inconsistent beliefs, he should be able to discover this *a priori* merely by examining his beliefs and their logical relations and by considering the meanings he attaches to the words in which he formulates his beliefs to others and to himself. But surely no amount of such *a priori* reflection will enable Pietro to discover any inconsistency here. Thus we seem forced back to our alternatives: Does he or does he not believe that London is beautiful? I do not think that there is a correct answer to Kripke's question because of the vagueness of our concept of belief. It is just not sufficiently clear when it applies. It is not clear enough what is entailed about a person's linguistic behavior by the claim that he believes or does not believe something. I accept Kripke's claim that the Italian-speakers who said (7) were justified in their assertion if people are ever justified in making claims about the beliefs of others, and the same applies to the English-speakers who said (8). But *we* have information that neither of these groups had, and, in view of this total information, we conclude that there is no correct answer 'yes' or 'no' to Kripke's question concerning Pietro's current state, "Does he believe that London is beautiful?" The criteria for the applicability of the concept of belief provide no answer in this rather complex case. These criteria do not draw a sharp boundary here, and this is an indication of the vagueness that infects our concept.

Kripke, in this paper, certainly makes no claim to be able to extend his theory of proper names so as to give an account of their behavior in contexts of assertion and belief. He maintains that this does not, however, throw the credibility of his earlier account into question. The view that belief-contexts present difficulties for his theory rests on an assumption that Kripke believes has not been established: the assumption that coreferential proper names are not intersubstitutive in belief-contexts. He attempts to establish this by the following strategy. "Rather I shall present—and this will form the core of the present paper—an argument for a paradox about names in belief-contexts that involves *no* principle of substitutivity. Instead it will be based on the principles—apparently so obvious that their use in these arguments is ordinarily tacit—of disquotation and translation" (Kripke, [PAB], p. 253). His argument seems to be that we could never establish that anyone ever believed that, e.g., Hesperus is the Evening Star and did not believe that Phosphorus is the Evening Star without applying the principles of disquotation and translation to what he says. Now Kripke claims that these two principles alone lead to his puzzle about Pietro. Since his puzzle has no apparent solution, the principles are shown to lead to paradoxical results and therefore they themselves are put into question.

In this book, the assumption that coreferential proper names are not intersubstitutive in belief-contexts has been used repeatedly. Is it really a dubious assumption? I do not think that Kripke's arguments show this at all. He argues for his conclusion by considering how we would ever know in a particular case that failure had occurred. But this is an empirical question. How do we know that the person A believes that p and does not believe that q? This is a question about the empirical criteria that are to be used in determining what a person believes. It is undoubtedly the case that these criteria are quite vague and not well understood. But surely we know without any consideration of them at all that belief-contexts are not Shakespearean. This is something we know *a priori*, through conceptual consideration. The argument is not that here and now we have before us a person who believes that $F(a)$ and does not believe that $F(b)$, even though

$a = b$. Rather, our claim is that, given our concepts of belief and assertion, we can surely coherently suppose that there could be such persons. There is nothing in the concepts with which we are concerned that prevents such a case from arising. We can grant this and still admit Kripke's point that any particular case we might actually confront, such as his example of Pietro, would be such that we could not conclusively establish that this was a case of failure of substitutivity. Kripke's argument seems to turn on a failure to separate this purely conceptual issue from the question of an adequate empirical test of belief. There really is no question that contexts of assertion and belief are both intensional and non-Shakespearean. That is involved in our understanding of these concepts.

Kripke rejects Frege's sense/reference distinction for proper names. He also rejects Russell's description-theory of names. Russell's and Frege's theories are the only theories that purport to offer a solution to Frege's puzzle. How does Kripke deal with it? How does 'Hesperus = Phosphorus' differ in cognitive value from 'Hesperus = Hesperus'? Kripke, of course, recognizes that these and other names may be introduced into our language with the aid of definite descriptions, e.g., by saying something like 'Hesperus is the first heavenly body to be seen in the evening sky during this time of the year'. The descriptions that are sometimes used to introduce proper names do not fix their meaning but only their reference. A principal reason for this conclusion, as we have seen, is just that if, e.g., the name 'Nixon' has its sense fixed by the description 'the winner of the 1968 presidential election', it would be a necessary truth that Nixon won the election. Similarly, if the name has its sense fixed by any other ordinary description, certain propositions would be necessary truths that ought to be contingent.

How then does Kripke deal with Frege's puzzle? Both 'Hesperus = Phosphorus' and 'Hesperus = Hesperus' are necessary truths, so the difference in their cognitive value must arise from the fact that the former of these is an *a posteriori* proposition and the latter an *a priori* one. What we discover when we learn that Hesperus = Phosphorus is that the alternative ways we use for fixing the reference of these names pick out the same planet. This way of putting the matter brings Kripke very close to Frege; for isn't the way the reference is fixed just sense? Kripke insists that it is not and accuses Frege of a confusion on the matter. He says,

> Frege should be criticized for using the term 'sense' in two senses. For he takes the sense of a designator to be its meaning; and he also takes it to be the way its reference is determined. Identifying the two, he supposes that both are given by definite descriptions. Ultimately, I will reject this second supposition too; but even were it right, I reject the first. A description may be used as synonymous with a designator, or it may be used to fix its reference. The two Fregean senses of 'sense' correspond to two senses of 'definition' in ordinary parlance. They should carefully be distinguished [Kripke, [NN], p. 59]

It is not Frege who is confused. For Frege, the principal function of sense is to determine reference. The determination of reference and the fixing of sense cannot, for him, be separated, as they are for Kripke. For Frege, the fixing of sense entails the fixing of reference. From his point of view, Kripke has made a mystery out of what it is to fix the reference of a name. Kripke tries to fill in this gap with the causal or "chain-of-communication" theory of reference. According to this theory a name, e.g., 'Socrates', is first given to an object by an act of dubbing. It is then handed down from speaker to speaker through a chain of communication until finally it reaches us: e.g., our teacher hands the name down to us by telling us that Socrates was the teacher of Plato.

Kripke remarks that, "Hartry Field has proposed that, for some of the purposes of Frege's theory, his notion of sense should be replaced by the chain which determines the reference" ([NN], n. 22 This sentence does not appear in Kripke's book [NN]). Kripke does not object to Field's proposal. At any rate, it has the advantage of providing Kripke with a candidate for a solution to Frege's puzzle. Remember that, for Frege, sense is a *cognitive* concept. Sense is what we *understand* when we know the meaning of a word or sentence. But then how plausible is Field's suggestion? It is utterly implausible. It cannot seriously be maintained that what I learn when I learn that Hesperus = Phosphorus is that two chains of communication, lasting over many centuries, which bring down to me the names 'Hesperus' and 'Phosphorus', both originated with an initial dubbing of the same object. The statement that Hesperus = Phosphorus is not about communication at all but simply and solely about the heavens. But whether this is right or wrong, this version of his theory is not in opposition to the sense-theory but rather to a particular proposal as to the nature of sense. Unless Kripke has some candidate for the office of sense (and this would be contrary to his announced program, which is to dispense with this notion), he has no solution for Frege's puzzle.

Further, Kripke's theory of names results in a new paradox, which is rather closely related to Frege's puzzle about identity but is a consequence of Kripke's attempt to avoid the conceptual apparatus that Frege used for solving his puzzle. According to Kripke's Millian view, names contribute only their denotations to the propositions that sentences containing them express. Consequently, substitution of codesignative names in modal contexts goes through, *salva veritate*. But now the puzzle for Kripke's view is this: The account of names that justifies their substitutivity in alethic modal contexts, *salva veritate*, seems, *prima facie*, to justify it in epistemic contexts as well.

It would seem that the role that sense plays in Frege's theory of meaning must be played, at least partially, by the chain of communication on Kripke's account. Frege's theory of reference makes reference indirect; it is routed through sense. In contrast, Russell's theory of logically proper names and Kripke's theory of ordinary proper names are theories of direct reference. Kripke's account is given in terms of the chain of communication. The name is given to an object by an act of dubbing. A chain, it is said, is only as strong as its weakest link. Let us examine the first link in this chain, for it is the weakest link. A name, according to this account, is given to an object by an act of dubbing. The theory offers no account whatever of this act of dubbing. It can't, in turn, be analyzed in terms of a chain of communication, for this act is the first link in the chain. In fact, the causal theory is a theory about how speakers acquire names; it is not an account of *naming* at all. That it leaves unexplained.

Appendix

The Theory of Types and Classes in *Principia Mathematica*

In this appendix I present observations, from the intensional point of view, about some technical features of the logical system of *Principia Mathematica*. This work has been criticized, and alterations have been suggested as improvements, by authors who have failed to consider the uses of *Principia* as a theory of intensional contexts. I will discuss Quine's proposed reformulation of *Principia*'s theory of classes in section I; in section II I will discuss another alteration in that theory, the one proposed by Carnap. In the next two sections I deal with axioms of reducibility: in section III, with their role in the theory of classes; in section IV, in connection with *Principia*'s resolution of the Liar Antinomy in its intensional form.

I

Quine's Reformulation of *Principia*

In "Whitehead and the Rise of Modern Logic" Quine objects to the treatment of classes as logical constructions in *Principia*. "To the nominalist temper, accordingly, the elimination of classes in favor of expressions is a congenial objective; and this is what Russell is sometimes believed to have done in 1908 when he showed how contexts ostensibly treating of classes could be construed as abbreviations of other expressions wherein reference is made only to 'propositional functions' " (Quine, [WRML], p. 21). Nominalists who find comfort in the *Principia* treatment of classes are deceiving themselves, because the required propositional functions are not expressions but things denoted by them, attributes. Confusion on this point results, perhaps, from Russell's tendency to ignore the distinction

between the use and mention of signs. Still, a nominalist interpretation of *Principia* can hardly withstand a sympathetic reading of
that text as well as Russell's other logical writings of the same period.
When Russell writes about the "ultimate logical furniture of the
world," he means to include propositional functions and propositions
along with individuals, and sentences, open and closed.

Russell provides a construction of classes out of attributes.
Classes obey a principle of extensionality—they are identical when
they have the same elements, but coextensive attributes may still
differ. Quine says, "It is precisely this difference, in fact, and nothing
more, that Russell's contextual definition of classes accommodates;
his is a technical construction enabling us to speak ostensibly of
identical classes by way of shorthand for discourse about coincident
but perhaps non-identical attributes" (ibid., p. 22). Quine regards
this procedure as wrong, for, as he sees it, Russell's definition rests
the clearer on the obscurer. Classes have a clear identity-condition,
while the identity-condition for propositional functions is left
unspecified in *Principia*. Quine concludes: "In any case there are no
specific attributes that can be proved in *Principia* to be true of just the
same things and yet to differ from one another. The theory of attributes receives no application, therefore, for which the theory of
classes would not have served. Once classes have been introduced,
attributes are scarcely mentioned again in the course of the three
volumes" (ibid.).

Quine then proposes the following reformulation of *Principia*'s
theory of classes. Replace the notation ϕx by the primitive notation
of membership, $x\epsilon\alpha$. Thus $(\exists\alpha)(x)(x\epsilon\alpha)$ replaces $(\exists\phi)(x)(\phi x)$.
Attributes—propositional functions in the intensional sense—
disappear from the range of values of the bound variables. The
notation of class abstraction $\hat{x}(\phi x)$ is to be introduced as a definite
description $(\imath\alpha)(x)(x\epsilon\alpha \equiv \phi x)$. One new axiom schema of compre-
hension has to be added, $E!\hat{x}\ (\phi x)$; "all other principles of the
Principia theory of classes would be forthcoming" (Quine, ibid., p.
23). The notation ϕx remains as a "dummy matrix" for convenience
of exposition, as above, but the serious attributional sense it has in
Principia is removed; for ϕ cannot occur in quantifiers or be used in
actual statements and matrices.

No doubt *Principia,* thus reformulated, delivers the same theorems it now contains; and this is the standard by which Quine wants us to judge his recommendations. But if we think of *Principia* as a language that, with the addition of individual and functional constants, is capable of expressing matters of physical and empirical fact, Quine's reformulated version has the severe disadvantage that it renders inoperative Russell's solutions to the puzzles his theory of meaning was designed to solve. For example, using Sx to mean 'x scottizes' and Wx to mean 'x writes *Waverley*', it is a matter of empirical fact that '$\hat{x}(Sx)$' and '$\hat{x}(Wx)$' are names of the same class. Now George IV knew that $\hat{x}(Sx) = \hat{x}(Sx)$, so we seem to be able to infer that George IV knew that $\hat{x}(Sx) = \hat{x}(Wx)$, which, as a matter of empirical fact, he did not.

Russell's construction of classes out of propositional functions provides a solution to this puzzle. It turns on treating $S\hat{x}$ and $W\hat{x}$ as coincident but different propositional functions, and it depends on an exploitation of the scope ambiguities that class abstracts induce in intensional contexts on the *Principia* treatment. (The details are given in chapter 4, above). Quine abandons this solution when he abandons propositional functions in the attributive sense. Further, on his account, variables that range over classes now come to occupy positions in quantifiers; classes are part of the ultimate furniture of the world. Hence, names of classes cannot be denied access to the identity-predicate. With this, as we saw in chapter 2, are generated new cases of Frege's puzzle.

Let us see how a Quineian treatment of one form of the puzzle fares. Let $\hat{x}(Sx)$ and $\hat{x}(Wx)$ be used with the same meaning as above. How, for Quine, can

(1) $\hat{x}(Sx) = \hat{x}(Wx)$

differ in cognitive value from the trivial identity

(2) $\hat{x}(Sx) = \hat{x}(Sx)$?

To be sure, both (1) and (2) involve definite descriptions on both sides of the sign of identity on Quine's account. But Wx and Sx denote nothing; they are merely *true of* the same individuals. I cannot find here the conceptual tools required to distinguish (1) from (2) as regards the nature of its informative content.

Quine would hardly regard this as a defect of his reformulated *Principia*, since he does not seek to provide a solution for Frege's puzzle. We observe only that his reformulation is unsatisfactory from this point of view. What Quine apparently fails to appreciate is that the *Principia* treatment of classes is not primarily designed to serve the purpose of ontological reduction. It can also be used in the analysis of intentional discourse and as a solution to some paradoxes associated with the intentional idiom. Russell does not emphasize the latter uses of his theory in *Principia*. Nevertheless, they are there.

II

Carnap's Reformulation of *Principia*'s Theory of Classes

Carnap also, for reasons quite different from Quine's, proposes a reformulation of *Principia*'s theory of classes. In *Meaning and Necessity* he proposes the following contextual definition of class abstraction:

33–1.　'..$\hat{x}(fx)$..'　for　'$(g)[(g \equiv f) \supset ..g..]$'.

This definition must be supplemented by a convention determining, in any given case, what the *scope* of the abstract (indicated by the dots) is to be. Carnap's convention is that the scope of the abstract is to be the smallest sentence or matrix *in primitive notation* containing the abstract. He wants to contrast this definition with Russell's, which, transcribed into Carnap's notation, is this:

33–2.　'..$\hat{z}(fz)$..'　for　'$(\exists g)[(g \equiv f) . ..g..]$'.

The main point of comparison is that Carnap's 33–1 construes a statement about a class $\hat{x}(fx)$ as a statement about all properties coincident with f, whereas Russell's 33–2 construes it as a statement about *some* property coincident with f. Carnap says, "Russell does not explain his reasons for the form of the definition chosen, except for saying, correctly, that the definiens ought to be extensional; this, however, is likewise the case if a universal quantifier is used, as in 33–1" (Carnap, [*MN*], p. 147).

Carnap observes that Russell's definition leads to "serious difficulties, which make it appear doubtful whether the definition fulfills the purpose intended" [ibid., pp. 147–48]. To see this, we suppose *Principia* supplemented with functional constants; for we wish to consider it as a language capable of expressing matters of empirical fact. Now consider these two sentences, which belong to *Principia,* thus enlarged:

(1) $(x)(Fx.Bx \equiv Hx)$; briefly, $F\hat{z} \,.\, B\hat{z} \equiv H\hat{z}$,
(2) $F \,.\, B \neq H$, or, in a style closer to *Principia,*
     $F\hat{x} \,.\, B\hat{z} \neq H\hat{z}$.

These sentences say that the property Featherless Biped and the property Human are (1) equivalent but (2) not identical; thus they are both true. We now consider two more sentences:

(3) $\hat{z}(Hz) = H\hat{z}$ and
(4) $\hat{z}(Hz) \neq H\hat{z}$.

These sentences are well formed in *Principia* (pp. 83–84). They "look like" contradictories, but they are *both* true on Russell's definition. (3) expands into

(5) $(\exists g)[g \equiv H \,.\, (g\hat{z} = H\hat{z})]$,

which follows by existential generalization from

$$H\hat{z} \equiv H\hat{z} \,.\, H\hat{z} = H\hat{z}.$$

Sentence (4) however, is also true, for it expands into

(6) $(\exists g)[(g \equiv H) \,.\, (g\hat{z} \neq H\hat{z})]$,

which follows from (1) and (2) by existential generalization on '$F\hat{z}.B\hat{z}$'. This result is correct only on a certain convention regarding the scope of the abstract in (4). "Here we have to take into consideration Russell's rule of context, according to which the smallest sentence or matrix in the actually given abbreviated notation is to be taken as corresponding to the left side in the definition 33–2" (Carnap, [*MN*], p. 149).

The "serious difficulty" that Carnap finds in the *Principia* definition 33–2, then, is that, according to this, (3) and (4) are both true although "they look like contradictories." They are, of course not contradictories, as can be seen when they are expanded according to 33–2 into (5) and (6). The difficulty is that "The class expressions should be such that they can be manipulated as if they were names of entities; and Russell seems to assume that this aim has been reached. Our result makes this assumption doubtful" (Carnap, ibid.).

If, instead of Russell's 33–2, we adopt Carnap's 33–1, everything seems to turn out all right. (3) is no longer provable. Since, on Carnap's convention, the abstract is to be eliminated only from the atomic contexts in primitive notation, (4) is expanded into the negation of (3) and we no longer have an apparent contradiction. (Carnap is assuming that *Principia* is further changed to include '=' as a primitive.) But there are still serious difficulties.

Carnap is certainly correct in saying that Russell's aim is to so construe class abstracts as to make them behave *as if* they were names of real entities. But Russell does not want to assume that classes *are* part of the ultimate furniture of the world. They do not fall within the range of values of the bound variables of *Principia*. But to treat an expression as if it were a name involves giving it access to the identity-predicate. As Quine has said, "No entity without identity." Hence if $\hat{x}(Hx)$ is to behave as a name, it must be true that

(7) $\hat{x}(Hx) = \hat{x}(Hx)$.

According to Carnap's 33–1, (7) may be expanded into

(8) $(g)(l)[g \equiv H .\supset: l \equiv H .\supset. l = g]$.

But (8) asserts the extensionality of predicates (propositional functions), and it is false on the intended interpretation of *Principia*. It obliterates all distinction between propositional functions and classes and makes the logical construction of the latter pointless. In any case, (7) interpreted as (8) is not provable in *Principia*. This is as it should be; for, if (7) is interpreted according to Carnap's definition 33–1, it is inconsistent with (1) and (2), which Carnap is supposing are both true. By instantiation, (8) entails

$$F.B \equiv H \supset: H \equiv H \supset. F.B = H,$$

which, by (1), together with $(x) (Hx \equiv Hx)$, entails

$$F.B = H,$$

which, together with (2), yields a contradiction. Since we desire to retain (1), (2), and (7)—as Carnap surely does as well—we must reject his proposed definition 33–1.

In the intended interpretation of (the first edition of) *Principia*, properties and relations are to be understood as intensional, not extensional entities on pain of undercutting Russell's solution to Frege's puzzle as well as his solution to what Carnap calls "the antinomy of the name-relation." On the other hand, Russell's definition 33–2 does deliver (7) as a theorem (immediately from *20·13) without forcing the extensionalization of propositional functions, as Carnap's definition does.

Further, Carnap's proof of the truth of (4) can be avoided by an alteration in *Principia*'s scope conventions for class abstracts. (4) is ambiguous as it stands. A scope indicator, such as is employed with definite descriptions, may be used to distinguish the alternative interpretations of (4) either as

$$(9) \quad \sim[\hat{z}(Hz)] \; \hat{z}(Hz) = H\hat{z}$$

or as

$$(10) \quad [\hat{z}(Hz)] \; \hat{z}(Hz) \neq H\hat{z}.$$

It is (9) that is the contradictory of (3), and it is provably false in *Principia;* for (9) expands, by Russell's definition, into the negation of (5). Carnap is quite correct in claiming that Russell's rule of context requires the elimination of the abstract in (4) from the smallest context in *abbreviated notation*. He cites *Principia,* page 173, to justify this. Russell says ([*PM*], p. 188) that, "with regard to the scope of $\hat{z}(\psi z)$, and to the order of elimination of two such expressions, we shall adopt the same conventions as were explained in *14 for $(\imath x)(\phi x)$." He says, further, "It will be found in practice that the scope usually required is the smallest proposition enclosed in dots or brackets in which '$(\imath x)(\phi x)$' occurs. Hence, when this scope is to be given to $(\imath x)(\phi x)$, we shall usually omit explicit mention of the scope" (ibid., p. 173).

Carnap has correctly applied the scope conventions explicitly given by Russell in *Principia*. The result is that (3) and (4) do look like contradictories, and, consequently, $\hat{z}(Hz)$ fails, to this extent, to behave like the name of a real object. But the fault is not with Russell's contextual definition of class abstraction. What is called for is a slight modification of Russell's scope conventions ([*PM*], p. 174), as follows (assuming, with Carnap, an altered *Principia,* with '$=$' as part of the primitive notation): *If no explicit scope operator occurs in the proposition, then let the scope of an abstract be the atomic context in the primitive notation containing the abstract. If under the same conditions two abstracts occur in an atomic context in the primitive notation, let the leftmost abstract have the larger scope.* Under this convention, (3) and (4) continue to "look like" contradictories, but the derivation of (4) from (1) and (2) would involve a simple scope fallacy.

III

Axioms of Reducibility and the Logical Construction of Classes

If classes are logical constructions, class names must behave like names of objects. Whatever else this entails, it must provide that class abstracts obey the standard laws of identity and, in particular, the law of the reflexivity of identity $\hat{x}(\phi x) = \hat{x}(\phi x)$. *Principia* yields the reflexivity of identity for class abstracts, but not without an essential use of the axioms of reducibility. Another constraint on an acceptable logical construction of classes is that, according to the construction, classes must be extensional; i.e., coextensive propositional functions must determine the same class. *Principia* provides the required extensionality, again with the aid of the axioms of reducibility. In his *Introduction to Mathematical Logic* Alonzo Church gives the following characterization of the contemporary view concerning the role of these axioms.

> The content of the axioms of reducibility is, for a propositional function of arbitrary level, that there exists a formally equivalent propositional function of the first level (the intended interpretation being such that the formal equivalence of propositional functions is not alone sufficient to render them identical). This has been much criticized, in particular on the ground that the effect is largely to restore the possibility of impredicative definition which the distinction of levels was designed to eliminate. Indeed, as many have urged, the true choice would seem to be between the simple functional calculi and the ramified functional calculi without axioms of reducibility. It is hard to think of a point of view from which the intermediate position represented by the ramified functional calculi with axioms of reducibility would appear to be significant. [Church, [*IML*], p. 355]

The system of the first edition of *Principia* is precisely that of ramified type theory with axioms of reducibility. Church here says that it is hard to think of a point of view from which it would appear to be significant. These observations were made in 1956. Twenty years later, in a paper entitled "Comparison of Russell's Resolution of the Semantical Antinomies with That of Tarski," Church records a change of view: "The effect of the axioms [of reducibility] is that . . . it is only in intension that we are to think of additional values of the functional variables as arising at each new level. Thus the rejection of impredicative definition is annulled in extensional but not in intensional matters" (Church, [CRRSAT], p. 758). He then suggests that this restoration of impredicative definition in extensional but not in intensional matters might be defended on the ground that there are antinomies that are intensional in character but not semantical. For example, Bouleus believes that he is sometimes mistaken. Suppose that none of his other beliefs *is* mistaken. Is Bouleus, or is he not, sometimes mistaken? Church now concludes that he was wrong in 1956 and that ". . . it is only by confining attention to extensional logic that it can be said that ramified type theory with axioms of reducibility has no interest as an intermediate position between pure ramified type theory and simple type theory" (ibid., n. 25).

Church here draws our attention to an intensional antinomy rather like the semantical antinomy of "The Liar." His remarks could as well have been supported by the so-called "antinomy of the name-relation" in its class form. The Russellian solution to this paradox turns on treating class abstracts as incomplete symbols, and it exploits the scope ambiguities such expressions induce in intensional contexts. Russell's theory of classes is embedded within the context of the ramified theory of types, and it gives a central role to the axioms of reducibility. Russell's contextual definition is

$$*20.1 \quad f\{\hat{z}(\psi z)\} \ .=: (\exists\phi) : \phi!x \ .\equiv_x .\psi x : f\{\phi!\hat{z}\} \quad \text{Df.}$$

The definition effects the logical construction of classes out of propositional functions. The essential property of classes is extensionality; classes are identical when they have the same members. To justify this definition, it must be shown, therefore, that it accords classes the necessary extensionality. The condition is stated in the theorem

$$*20.15. \quad \vdash:. \ \psi x \equiv_x \chi x :\equiv. \ \hat{z}(\psi z) = \hat{z}(\chi z).$$

What is to be noted, for our purposes, is the use of *12.1, an axiom of reducibility, in the proof of *20.15. If the contextual definition of class abstracts itself gains part of its interest from the point of view of intensional logic, as we have argued, it is the case that from this point of view there is significance in the ramified theory of types with the axiom of reducibility, whose use seems unavoidable in the proof of *20.15. Note again that *20.15 immediately implies

$$\hat{x}(\phi x) = \hat{x}(\phi x),$$

reflexivity of identity for classes. This must be provable if abstracts are to behave as names of objects, as is intended. But the axioms of reducibility are again unavoidable in the proof of this theorem and of others that have the effect of yielding the conditions that are necessary if class abstracts are to serve their function as incomplete symbols whose behavior is sufficiently like that of genuine names of objects to justify the claim that the logical construction of classes has been effected (Whitehead and Russell [*PM*], p. 78). This is the answer to Carnap's question as to why Russell's definition *20.01 takes its existential form. Carnap says, "Russell does not explain his reasons for the form of the definition chosen" (Carnap, [*MN*], p. 14). The reason, however, is clear. In this form the definition contains the case of an axiom of reducibility required for the logical construction of classes. This is what Russell means when he says, in *Introduction to Mathematical Philosophy,* "The axiom of reducibility involves all that is really essential in the theory of classes" (Russell, [*IMP*], p. 191), and, again, "The theory of classes, as above outlined, reduces itself to one axiom and one definition" (ibid., p. 193).

Comparing $[(\imath x)(\phi x)]$ and $[\hat{x}(\phi x)]$

Summarizing his introductory account of incomplete symbols, Russell ([*PM*], p. 83) indicates the principal ways in which the incompleteness of definite descriptions and class abstracts manifests itself within *Principia,* and he draws a comparison between these two kinds of incomplete symbols. Concerning $(\imath x)(\phi x)$, the chief way in which its incompleteness is relevant, he says, is that we do not have

$$(x) \cdot fx \cdot \supset \cdot f(\imath x)(\phi x).$$

$f(\imath x)(\phi x)$ is not a value of $f\hat{x}$, so that, even when all values of $f\hat{x}$ are true, $f(\imath x)(\phi x)$ may not be true. This is the case only when $(\imath x)(\phi x)$ does not exist. On the other hand,

$$(x) : fx \cdot E!(\imath x)(\phi x) :\supset \cdot f(\imath x)(\phi x),$$

is a theorem of *Principia.* This special case can be generalized, and Russell says, "As soon as we know $E!(\imath x)(\phi x)$, the fact that $(\imath x)(\phi x)$ is an incomplete symbol becomes irrelevant so long as we confine ourselves to truth-functions of whatever proposition is its scope"

(*PM*, p. 83). He then adds the important observation, "But even when E!$(\imath x)(\phi x)$, the incompleteness of $(\imath x)(\phi x)$ may be relevant when we pass outside truth-functions." The first observation—that the incompleteness of $(\imath x)(\phi x)$ is irrelevant when E!$(\imath x)(\phi x)$, as long as we confine ourselves to truth-functions—is a theorem of *Principia*,

$$*14.3. \quad \vdash:. \; p \equiv q \;.\supset_{p,\,q} . \; f(p) \equiv f(q) : E!(\imath x)(\phi x) :\supset:$$
$$f\{[(\imath x)(\phi x)] \;.\; \chi(\imath x)(\phi x) \;.\equiv.\; [(\imath x)(\phi x)] \;.$$
$$f\{\chi(\imath x)(\phi x)\}.$$

The theorem entails that the scope ambiguities induced by definite descriptions can be ignored when $(\imath x)(\phi x)$ occurs in an extensional context, provided E!$(\imath x)(\phi x)$. Suppose that, as in Frege's treatment of descriptions, they always denote, if only because an arbitrary object is assigned as the denotation of $(\imath x)(\phi x)$ in case $\sim(\exists c)(x)(\phi x \equiv x = c)$. Then scope distinctions for descriptions can be ignored as long as we confine ourselves to extensional contexts in such a theory. Further, this Fregean treatment of descriptions would seem to be the better one, because it is able to ignore the whole matter of scope and the apparatus of scope operators, which play such an important role in the Russellian account. Another way of putting the point is to say that the distinctively Russellian treatment of definite descriptions, as opposed to the alternative Fregean account, is unmotivated except from the point of view of the needs of an account of intensional contexts. (Details are given in chapter 4, above.)

By comparison, the incompleteness of class abstracts manifests itself rather differently. The following is true, though not proved in *Principia* (we use Russell's scope operator for class abstracts, $[\hat{x}(\phi x)]$, which is to be used like its analogue, $[(\imath x)(\phi x)]$, for definite descriptions):

$$\vdash:. \; p \equiv q \;.\supset_{p.q} . \; f(p) \equiv f(q) :\supset: f\{[\hat{x}(\phi x)] \;.\; \chi\hat{x}(\phi x)\} \;.\equiv.$$
$$[\hat{x}(\phi x)]f\{\chi\hat{x}(\phi x)\}.$$

What this theorem asserts is that the scope of a class abstract can be taken to be either large or small without affecting the truth-value of the proposition containing the abstract as long as the context containing it is extensional. This theorem is the analogue for class abstracts of *14.3 for definite descriptions, except that *14.3 has the condition $E!(\imath x)(\phi x)$, the analogue for which, $(\exists\psi)(\psi!x .\equiv_x . \phi x)$, is missing in the theorem about class abstraction. This is an axiom of reducibility; hence its presence in the antecedent of a conditional would be vacuous. This explains (cf. *PM,* p. 80), the absence of the scope operator for abstracts in the theorems of *Principia.* It is because *Principia* is intended primarily as a study in "the principles of mathematics," an area free of the intentional idiom. Furthermore, there is no analogue for class abstracts, of improper descriptions. As Russell says, "We may say generally that the fact that $\hat{z}(\phi z)$ is an incomplete symbol is not relevant so long as we confine ourselves to extensional functions of functions, but is apt to become relevant for other functions of functions" (*PM,* p. 84). Again, as with definite descriptions, this amounts to the recognition that the peculiarly Russellian treatment of classes as logical constructions is motivated only from the intensional point of view.

IV

Axioms of Reducibility and the Intensional Liar

In this entire section I adhere very closely to John Myhill's "A Refutation of an Unjustified Attack on the Axiom of Reducibility" (Myhill, [RUAAR]). My aim is to explain how the system of the ramified theory of types, together with axioms of reducibility, contained in the first edition of *Principia Mathematica* excludes intensional antinomies.

According to a tradition that begins with Ramsey, the antinomies, which have played such a large role in the development of logic and set theory during this century, fall into two distinct classes. One group of antinomies is logical or set-theoretical. This group includes Russell's antinomy, Burali-Forti's antinomy of the greatest ordinal, and Cantor's antinomy of the greatest cardinal. The other group of antinomies is distinguished as "semantical." It includes the Epimenides ("The Liar"), the antinomy concerning "heterological" predicates, and the one concerning the least integer not namable in fewer than nineteen syllables, as well as the Richard antinomy. What Ramsey noticed was that the members of the second group all make crucial use of "linguistic" or semantical concepts, such as denoting, truth (as a predicate of *sentences*), and definability (as a binary semantical relation). The logical or set-theoretical antinomies, on the other hand, use only the vocabulary of logic and set theory. Ramsey concluded that, since the semantical antinomies could not even be formulated without adding semantics to the language of logic and set theory, there was no need for the complexities of the ramified theory of types, which were designed to deal with these linguistic problems. He observed that the simple theory of types was enough to exclude the known logical and set-theoretical antinomies and that the complexities of ramification were, from the point of view of the requirements of logic, unnecessary. Subsequently, Tarski showed how to eliminate semantical antinomies by means of the strict observation of the distinction between object and metalanguage, together with the prohibition of "semantical closure" (languages may not contain their own semantics on pain of contradiction).

From the point of view of the present work, this classification is inadequate, because I wish to recognize antinomies that are neither logical, set-theoretical, nor semantical. In particular, I shall now turn my attention to the intensional version of the Epimenides, which can be formulated without use of semantical concepts but which, since it does make use of the concepts of *proposition* and *assertion,* falls outside the sphere of the purely extensional. My aim is to recover the point of view that led Russell to introduce the complexities of the ramified theory of types in the first place. To do this, I present an antinomy that cannot be resolved either by the simple theory of types or by the exclusion of semantical closure (the hierarchy of languages). It is an example of an intensional antinomy.

The Intensional Liar. Let E be the set of all *propositions* asserted by Epimenides. We shall suppose E to have but one member. This is the proposition that all elements of E are false. Myhill provides the following proof of inconsistency within the simple theory of types. We assume

$$(1) \quad p \epsilon E \; . \equiv . \; p = (q)(q \epsilon E \supset \sim q).$$

We abbreviate $(q)(q \epsilon E \supset \sim q)$ by $\mathfrak{E}$. The two parts of the contradiction then follow: Assume $\mathfrak{E}$; then

(2)	$(q)(q\epsilon E \supset \sim q)$,	
(3)	$p\epsilon E \mathrel{.}\equiv\mathrel{.} p = \mathfrak{E}$,	from (1)
(4)	$\mathfrak{E}\epsilon E$,	from (3)
(5)	$\mathfrak{E}\epsilon E \supset \sim\mathfrak{E}$;	from (2)
∴ (6)	$\sim\mathfrak{E}$.	from (4) and (5)

Assume, conversely, $\sim\mathfrak{E}$; then

(7)	$(\exists q)(q\epsilon E \mathrel{.} q)$.	definition of $\mathfrak{E}$

Let q_0 be such a q; then

(8)	$q_0\epsilon E$,	
(9)	q_0,	
(10)	$q_0\epsilon E \mathrel{.}\equiv\mathrel{.} q_0 = \mathfrak{E}$,	from (1)
(11)	$q_0 = \mathfrak{E}$;	from (8) and (10)
∴ (12)	$\mathfrak{E}$.	from (9) and (11)

Thus the assumption (1) leads to a contradiction within simple type theory. This assumption cannot, however, even be formulated within the ramified theory of types. The ramified theory admits of alternative formulations, and Whitehead and Russell themselves offer different versions in the Introduction, in chapter 2, and in *12 of the first edition of *Principia*. Another version is given by Church in his "Comparison of Russell's Resolution of the Semantical Antinomies with that of Tarski" (Church [CRRSAT]). Myhill's version is given in the work cited at the beginning of this section. (Myhill, in turn, has followed Schütte's *Beweistheorie* [Berlin: Springer Verlag, 1960].)

Some informal remarks will, perhaps, help the reader to see the underlying error upon which, according to the ramified theory of types, the antinomy of the intensional liar rests. Ramification is introduced into simple type theory in order to avoid "vicious-circle fallacies." One form of vicious-circle "fallacy" occurs when an object is defined with the use of a quantifier that includes that very object within its range. Definitions that commit the "fallacy" are called "impredicative." Church gives the following elegant formulation of the requirement of predicativity: "To avoid impredicativity the essential restriction is that quantification over any domain (type) must not be allowed to add new members to the domain, as it is held that adding new members changes the meaning of quantification over the domain in such a way that a vicious circle results" (Church, [CRRSAT], p. 747). This is what occurs in the definition of the class E in (1), above. The proposition 𝔈 is specified with the use of quantification over all propositions, including, necessarily, 𝔈 itself.

Bibliography

All works cited in my text are listed. Abbreviated titles used in my citations appear in square brackets immediately following the author's name.

Anderson, C. A. [SNALSD] "Some New Axioms for the Logic of Sense and Denotation." *Nous* 14, no. 2 (1980): 217–34.

Barcan, R. C. (Ruth Barcan Marcus). [FCFOSI] "A Functional Calculus of First Order Based on Strict Implication." *Journal of Symbolic Logic* 2 (1946): 1–16.

Bell, David. [*FTJ*] *Frege's Theory of Judgement*. Oxford: Oxford University Press, 1979.

Carnap, Rudolf. [*IS*] *Introduction to Semantics*. Cambridge, Mass.: Harvard University Press, 1942.

———. [MQ] "Modalities and Quantification." *Journal of Symbolic Logic* 11 (1946): 33–64.

———. [*MN*] *Meaning and Necessity: A Study in Semantics and Modal Logic*. Chicago: University of Chicago Press, 1947.

Caton, C. E., ed. [*POL*] *Philosophy and Ordinary Language*. Urbana: University of Illinois Press, 1963.

Church, Alonzo. [Review Q] Review of "Notes on Existence and Necessity" by W. V. O. Quine. *Journal of Symbolic Logic* 8, no. 2 (1943): 45–47.

———. [Review C] Review of *Introduction to Semantics* by Rudolf Carnap. *Philosophical Review* 52 (1943): 298–304.

———. [Abstract] Abstract of "A Formulation of the Logic of Sense and Denotation." *Journal of Symbolic Logic* 2 (1946): 31.

———. [CASAB] "On Carnap's Analysis of Statements of Assertion and Belief." *Analysis* 10, no. 5 (1950): 97–99.

————. [NAESA] "The Need for Abstract Entities in Semantic Analysis." *Proceedings of the American Academy of Arts and Sciences* 60, no. 1 (1951): 100–112. Reprinted in J. J. Katz and J. A. Fodor, eds., *The Structure of Language* (see below). (Page numbers cited in my references to NAESA are to the Katz and Fodor volume.)

————. [FLSD] "A Formulation of the Logic of Sense and Denotation." In Paul Henle, H. M. Kallen, and S. K. Langer, eds., *Structure, Method, and Meaning: Essays in Honor of Henry M. Sheffer.* New York: Liberal Arts Press, 1951.

————. [IIIB] "Intensional Isomorphism and Identity of Belief." *Philosophical Studies* 5 (1954): 65–73.

————. [IML] *Introduction to Mathematical Logic,* vol. 1. Princeton, Princeton University Press, 1956.

————. [LA] "Logic and Analysis." *Atti del XII Congresso Internazionale di Filosofia,* vol. 4, pp. 76–81. Florence: Sansoni, 1960.

————. [Postscript 1968] "Postscript 1968." Postscript to Church's [Review Q]. Spanish translation by T. M. Simpson. In T. M. Simpson, ed., *Semántica filosófica: Problemas y discusiones.* Buenos Aires: Siglo XXI Argentina Editores, 1973.

————. [RSTT] "Russellian Simple Type Theory." *Preceedings and Addresses of the American Philosophical Association* 57 (1973–74): 21–33.

————. [CRRSAT] "Comparison of Russell's Resolution of the Semantical Antinomies with That of Tarski." *Journal of Symbolic Logic* 41, no. 4 (1976): 747–60.

————. [HFCFIL] "How Far Can Frege's Intensional Logic Be Represented within Russell's Theory of Descriptions?" Unpublished abstract of an address presented to the American Philosophical Association, San Diego, April, 1979.

————. [RCQP] "A Remark concerning Quine's Paradox about Modality." Forthcoming in *Sintaxis* (Montevideo).

Davidson, Donald. [TMLL] "Theories of Meaning and Learnable Languages." In *Proceedings of the 1964 International Congress for Logic, Methodology, and Philosophy of Science,* edited by Yehoshua Bar-Hillel. Amsterdam: North-Holland Publishing Co., 1965.

————, and Hintikka, Jaakko, eds. [W&O] *Words and Objections:*

Essays on the Work of W. V. Quine. Dordrecht, Holland: D. Reidel Publishing Co., 1969.

Dummett, Michael. [*Frege*] *Frege: Philosophy of Language*. London: Duckworth, 1973.

Føllesdal, Dagfinn. [IQ] "Interpretation of Quantifiers." In *Proceedings of the Third International Congress for Logic, Methodology, and Philosophy of Science* (Amsterdam 1967), edited by B. van Rootselaar and J. F. Staal. Amsterdam: North-Holland Publishing Co., 1968.

Frege, Gottlob. [*FFG*] and [*TPWGF*]: English translations of *Begriffsschrift, eine der arithmetischen nachgebildete Formelsprache des reinen Denkens*. Halle: Verlag von L. Nebert, 1879. For [*FFG*], see van Heijenoort, Jan. For [*TPWGF*], see below.

———. [*FA*] *The Foundations of Arithmetic: A logico-mathematical enquiry into the concept of number*. English translation of *Die Grundlagen der Arithmetik, eine logisch-mathematische Untersuchung über den Begriff der Zahl* (Breslau: Verlag von Wilhelm Koebner, 1884). Translated by J. L. Austin. Oxford: Basil Blackwell, 1959.

———. [SR] "On Sense and Reference." In Frege, [*TPWGF*].

———. [*TPWGF*] *Translations from the Philosophical Writings of Gottlob Frege*. Edited and translated by Max Black and Peter Geach. Oxford: Basil Blackwell, 1952.

———. [*PMC*] *Philosophical and Mathematical Correspondence of Gottlob Frege*. Edited by Brian McGuinness. Translated by Hans Kaal. Chicago: University of Chicago Press, 1980.

———. [*WB*] *Wissenschaftlicher Briefwechsel*. Edited by G. Gabriel, H. Hermes, F. Kambartel, C. Thiel, and A. Veraart. Hamburg: Felix Meiner Verlag, 1976.

Hintikka, Jaakko. [*KB*] *Knowledge and Belief: An Introduction to the Logic of the Two Notions*. Ithaca: Cornell University Press, 1962.

———. [KBLC] "Knowledge, Belief, and Logical Consequence." *Ajatus* 32 (1970): 25–31.

———. [IPWV] "Impossible Possible Worlds Vindicated." *Journal of Philosophical Logic* 4, no. 4 (1975): 475–84.

Kaplan, David. [*FIL*] *Foundations of Intensional Logic*. Ann Arbor, Mich.: University Microfilms, 1964.

Katz, J. J., and Fodor, J. A., eds. *The Structure of Language*. Englewood Cliffs, N.J.: Prentice-Hall, 1964.

Kripke, Saul. [NN] "Naming and Necessity." In Donald Davidson and Gilbert Harman, eds., *Semantics and Natural Languages*. Dordrecht, Holland: D. Reidel Publishing Co., 1972.

———. [Preface *NN*] *Naming and Necessity*. Reprint of [NN], with corrections and a new Preface. Cambridge, Mass.: Harvard University Press, 1980.

———. "A Puzzle about Belief." In Avishai Margalit, ed., *Meaning and Use: Papers Presented at the Second Jerusalem Philosophical Encounter, April 1976*. Dordrecht, Holland: D. Reidel Publishing Co., 1979.

Linsky, Leonard, ed. [*SPL*] *Semantics and the Philosophy of Language*. Urbana: University of Illinois Press, 1952.

———. [RR] "Reference and Referents." In C. E. Caton, ed., *Philosophy and Ordinary Language*. Urbana: University of Illinois Press, 1963.

———. [SD] "Substitutivity and Descriptions." *Journal of Philosophy* 63, no. 21 (1966): 673–83.

———. [IDL] "On Interpreting Doxastic Logic." *Journal of Philosophy* 65, no. 17 (1968): 500–502.

———, ed. [*RM*] *Reference and Modality*. Oxford: Oxford University Press, 1971.

———. [*ND*] *Names and Descriptions*. Chicago: University of Chicago Press, 1977. Corrected paperback ed., 1980.

———. [BN] "Believing and Necessity." *Proceedings and Addresses of the American Philosophical Association* 47 (1977): 526–538. Reprinted, with corrections, in *Decision and Theory* 11 (1979): 81–94.

Marcus, Ruth Barcan. See Barcan, R. C.

Myhill, John. [USNNRP] "The Undefinability of the Set of Natural Numbers in the Ramified *Principia*." In George Nakhnikian, ed., *Bertrand Russell's Philosophy*. London: Duckworth, 1974.

———. [RUAAR] "A Refutation of an Unjustified Attack on the Axiom of Reducibility." In G. W. Roberts, ed., *Bertrand Russell Memorial Volume*. London: Allen & Unwin, 1979.

Parsons, Charles. [FTN] "Frege's Theory of Number." In Max Black ed., *Philosophy in America*. Ithaca: Cornell University Press, 1965.

Parsons, Terence. [FHIS] "Frege's Hierarchies of Indirect Senses and the Paradox of Analysis." In P. French, T. Uehling, and H. Wettstein, eds., *Midwest Studies in Philosophy,* vol. 6. Minneapolis: University of Minnesota Press, 1981.

Putnam, Hilary. [MM] "The Meaning of 'Meaning'." In Keith Gunderson, ed., *Minnesota Studies in the Philosophy of Science,* vol. 7. Minneapolis: University of Minnesota Press, 1975.

Quine, W. V. O. [WRML] "Whitehead and the Rise of Modern Logic." In P. A. Schilpp, ed., *The Philosophy of Alfred North Whitehead,* Library of Living Philosophers, vol. 5. Evanston and Chicago: Northwestern University Press, 1941. Reprinted in W. V. O. Quine, *Selected Logic Papers* [*SLP*]. (Page numbers cited in my text are to *SLP.*)

———. [NEN] "Notes on Existence and Necessity." *Journal of Philosophy* 40 (1943): 113–27. Reprinted in L. Linsky, ed., [*SPL*], *Semantics and the Philosophy of Language.* (Page numbers cited in my text are to *SPL.*)

———. [*FLPV*] *From a Logical Point of View: 9 Logico-Philosophical Essays.* 1st ed. Cambridge, Mass.: Harvard University Press, 1953. 2d rev. ed., 1961; 3d rev. ed., 1980. (Page numbers cited in my text are to the third edition.)

———. [RM] "Reference and Modality." In Quine [*FLPV*]. Reprinted in L. Linsky, ed., *Reference and Modality* [*RM*]. (Page numbers cited in my text are to *RM.*)

———. [TGMI] "Three Grades of Modal Involvement." *Proceedings of the XIth International Congress of Philosophy, Brussels, 1953,* vol. 14. Amsterdam: North-Holland Publishing Co., 1953. Reprinted in Quine, *The Ways of Paradox and Other Essays* [*WP*]. (Citations of TGMI in my text are to page numbers of the second edition of *WP.*)

———. [QPA] "Quantifiers and Propositional Attitudes." In Quine [*WP*].

———. [*WO*] *Word and Object.* Cambridge, Mass.: MIT Press, 1960.

———. [*SLP*] *Selected Logic Papers.* New York: Random House, 1966.

———. [*WP*] *The Ways of Paradox and Other Essays.* 1st ed. Cambridge, Mass.: Harvard University Press, 1966. 2d ed., rev. and enl., 1976. (Citations in my text are to page numbers of the second edition of *WP*.)

Rawls, John. [*TJ*] *A Theory of Justice*. Cambridge, Mass.: Harvard University Press, 1971.

Russell, Bertrand. [*PoM*] *Principles of Mathematics*. 2d ed. New York: Norton, n.d.

———. [OD] "On Denoting." *Mind* n.s. 14 (1905): 479–93. Reprinted in Bertrand Russell, *Logic and Knowledge: Essays 1901–1950,* edited by R. C. Marsh. London: Allen & Unwin, 1958.

———. [*IMP*] *Introduction to Mathematical Philosophy*. 2d ed. London: Allen & Unwin, 1920.

———. [ISE*PM*] *Introduction to the Second Edition*. In Alfred North Whitehead and Bertrand Russell, *Principia Mathematica,* 2d ed., vol. 1. Cambridge, Eng.: At the University Press, 1925.

———. See Whitehead, A. N., and Russell, Bertrand.

Smullyan, A. F. [MD] "Modality and Description." *Journal of Symbolic Logic* 13, no. 1 (1948): 31–37. Reprinted in Leonard Linsky, ed., *Reference and Modality* [*RM*]. (Citations in my text are to page numbers of [MD].)

Schütte, Kurt. *Beweistheorie*. Berlin; Springer Verlag, 1960.

Tarski, Alfred. [CTFL] "The Concept of Truth in Formalized Languages." In Alfred Tarski, *Logic, Semantics, Metamathematics*. Oxford: Oxford University Press, 1956.

van Heijenoort, Jan, ed. [*FFG*] *From Frege to Gödel: A Source Book in Mathematical Logic, 1879–1931*. Cambridge, Mass.: Harvard University Press, 1967.

Whitehead, A. N., and Russell, Bertrand. [*PM*] *Principia Mathematica,* vol. 1. 1st ed. Cambridge, Eng.: At the University Press, 1910. 2d ed., 1925.

Wittgenstein, Ludwig. [*TLP*] *Tractatus Logico-Philosophicus*. Translated by David Pears and B. F. McGuinness. London: Routledge & Kegan Paul. 1961.

———. [*PI*] *Philosophical Investigations*. Translated by G. E. M. Anscombe. Oxford: Basil Blackwell, 1953.

Wu, K. G. J. [HD] "Hintikka and Defensibility." *Ajatus* 32 (1970): 25–31.

Index

Index